DOCKER: ZERO TO HERO

BUILD, TEST, AND DEPLOY APPLICATIONS FAST

4 BOOKS IN 1

BOOK 1
DOCKER DEMYSTIFIED: A BEGINNER'S GUIDE TO CONTAINERIZATION

BOOK 2
MASTERING DOCKER: ADVANCED TECHNIQUES AND BEST PRACTICES

BOOK 3
DOCKER DEPLOYMENT STRATEGIES: SCALING AND ORCHESTRATING CONTAINERS

BOOK 4
EXPERT DOCKER: BUILDING COMPLEX MICROSERVICES ARCHITECTURES

ROB BOTWRIGHT

Copyright © 2024 by Rob Botwright
All rights reserved. No part of this book may be reproduced or transmitted in any form or by any means, electronic or mechanical, including photocopying, recording, or by any information storage and retrieval system, without permission in writing from the publisher.

Published by Rob Botwright
Library of Congress Cataloging-in-Publication Data
ISBN 978-1-83938-698-5
Cover design by Rizzo

Disclaimer

The contents of this book are based on extensive research and the best available historical sources. However, the author and publisher make no claims, promises, or guarantees about the accuracy, completeness, or adequacy of the information contained herein. The information in this book is provided on an "as is" basis, and the author and publisher disclaim any and all liability for any errors, omissions, or inaccuracies in the information or for any actions taken in reliance on such information. The opinions and views expressed in this book are those of the author and do not necessarily reflect the official policy or position of any organization or individual mentioned in this book. Any reference to specific people, places, or events is intended only to provide historical context and is not intended to defame or malign any group, individual, or entity. The information in this book is intended for educational and entertainment purposes only. It is not intended to be a substitute for professional advice or judgment. Readers are encouraged to conduct their own research and to seek professional advice where appropriate. Every effort has been made to obtain necessary permissions and acknowledgments for all images and other copyrighted material used in this book. Any errors or omissions in this regard are unintentional, and the author and publisher will correct them in future editions.

BOOK 1 - DOCKER DEMYSTIFIED: A BEGINNER'S GUIDE TO CONTAINERIZATION

BOOK 2 - MASTERING DOCKER: ADVANCED TECHNIQUES AND BEST PRACTICES

BOOK 3 - DOCKER DEPLOYMENT STRATEGIES: SCALING AND ORCHESTRATING CONTAINERS

BOOK 4 - EXPERT DOCKER: BUILDING COMPLEX MICROSERVICES ARCHITECTURES

Introduction

Welcome to the "Docker: Zero to Hero" book bundle, a comprehensive guide designed to equip you with the knowledge and skills needed to become a proficient Docker user and accelerate your journey from novice to expert in containerization. In today's fast-paced world of software development and deployment, Docker has emerged as a fundamental tool for building, testing, and deploying applications with speed, efficiency, and scalability. Whether you're just starting with Docker or looking to master advanced techniques for managing complex microservices architectures, this book bundle has something for everyone.

The bundle comprises four meticulously crafted books, each covering a distinct aspect of Docker and containerization:

Book 1 - "Docker Demystified: A Beginner's Guide to Containerization": In this introductory book, readers will embark on a journey to demystify Docker and understand the core concepts of containerization. From Docker basics to creating and managing containers, this book provides a solid foundation for beginners to kickstart their Docker journey with confidence.

Book 2 - "Mastering Docker: Advanced Techniques and Best Practices": Building upon the foundational knowledge gained in Book 1, this book delves deeper into Docker's advanced features and best practices. Readers will learn how to optimize Docker images, implement networking and storage solutions, and orchestrate multi-container applications using Docker Compose. With a focus on scalability, security, and performance, this book equips readers with the expertise to leverage Docker effectively in production environments.

Book 3 - "Docker Deployment Strategies: Scaling and Orchestrating Containers": Scaling and orchestrating containers at scale is a critical aspect of modern application deployment. In this book, readers will explore various deployment strategies, from setting up Docker Swarm clusters to implementing rolling updates and service scaling. Advanced networking and security considerations for deploying Docker in production are also covered, ensuring readers are well-prepared to handle real-world deployment scenarios.

Book 4 - "Expert Docker: Building Complex Microservices Architectures": Microservices architecture has become the de facto standard for building modern, scalable applications. In this advanced book, readers will learn how to architect and deploy complex, distributed systems using Docker. With a focus on designing scalable, resilient, and maintainable microservices architectures, this book equips readers with the knowledge and tools to tackle the challenges of building and managing sophisticated containerized applications.

Whether you're a beginner looking to grasp the fundamentals of Docker or an experienced practitioner aiming to optimize your Docker workflows and architect complex microservices architectures, this book bundle provides the guidance and expertise you need to succeed. Get ready to embark on a transformative journey into the world of Docker, where you'll learn to build, test, and deploy applications faster and more efficiently than ever before.

BOOK 1

DOCKER DEMYSTIFIED

A BEGINNER'S GUIDE TO CONTAINERIZATION

ROB BOTWRIGHT

Chapter 1: Introduction to Containerization

Evolution of Software Deployment traces a journey of technological advancements, reshaping the landscape of application delivery. It encompasses a rich tapestry of methodologies, from the early days of manual installations to the sophisticated automation frameworks prevalent today.

In the nascent stages, software deployment involved labor-intensive processes, with installations conducted manually on individual machines. Each software update required meticulous attention, as system administrators painstakingly traversed through installation wizards or executed commands to update applications. The process was time-consuming and error-prone, often leading to inconsistencies across environments.

With the advent of package managers, such as apt-get in Debian-based systems or yum in Red Hat-based systems, the deployment process became more streamlined. Package managers facilitated the installation and management of software packages, resolving dependencies automatically and ensuring uniformity across deployments. Users could simply execute commands like **apt-get install <package-name>** to deploy software effortlessly, significantly reducing deployment overhead.

The evolution of virtualization technologies further revolutionized software deployment practices. Virtual machines enabled the encapsulation of entire application environments, including the operating system, libraries, and dependencies, into portable entities. Tools like VMware and VirtualBox empowered developers to create, deploy, and manage isolated environments, fostering consistency and reproducibility in software deployments.

Containerization emerged as a game-changer in the realm of software deployment, offering lightweight, portable, and self-contained units for application delivery. Docker, with its intuitive CLI commands and declarative Dockerfiles, democratized containerization, enabling developers to package their applications and dependencies into immutable containers. The simplicity and efficiency of Docker accelerated the adoption of containerization, ushering in a new era of DevOps practices and continuous delivery pipelines.

Orchestration platforms like Kubernetes emerged to manage the complexities of deploying and scaling containerized applications. Kubernetes abstracted away the underlying infrastructure, providing robust scheduling, scaling, and service discovery capabilities. Through CLI commands like **kubectl apply -f <deployment-file.yaml>**, developers could deploy and manage their applications effortlessly, while operators could ensure high availability and resilience of the infrastructure.

Continuous Integration/Continuous Deployment (CI/CD) pipelines became integral to modern software deployment workflows. CI/CD tools like Jenkins, GitLab CI/CD, and CircleCI automated the build, test, and deployment processes, enabling rapid iteration and delivery of software updates. Developers could commit code changes to version control systems like Git, triggering automated pipelines that build, test, and deploy applications to production environments seamlessly.

Serverless computing emerged as a paradigm shift in software deployment, abstracting away infrastructure management entirely. Platforms like AWS Lambda, Azure Functions, and Google Cloud Functions allowed developers to focus solely on writing code, without worrying about server provisioning or scaling. Through CLI commands or graphical interfaces, developers could deploy functions that automatically scale based on demand, optimizing cost and resource utilization.

As technology continues to evolve, software deployment methodologies evolve in tandem, driven by the need for agility, scalability, and reliability. From manual installations to containerized microservices running on orchestrated platforms, the evolution of software deployment reflects a relentless pursuit of efficiency and innovation in the ever-changing landscape of software development.

Benefits of Containerization are manifold,

revolutionizing the landscape of software development and deployment. Containerization, epitomized by technologies like Docker, Kubernetes, and container orchestration platforms, offers a plethora of advantages, driving widespread adoption across industries.

Containers provide lightweight, portable, and self-contained units for packaging applications and their dependencies, ensuring consistency and reproducibility across different environments. With containerization, developers can encapsulate their applications, libraries, and configurations into immutable containers, eliminating the dreaded "it works on my machine" scenario. Through simple CLI commands like **docker build** and **docker run**, developers can create, deploy, and manage containers effortlessly, streamlining the development process.

One of the key benefits of containerization is its ability to facilitate microservices architecture, enabling the decomposition of monolithic applications into smaller, modular components. Microservices, deployed as independent containers, promote agility, scalability, and resilience, allowing teams to develop, deploy, and scale services independently. With container orchestration platforms like Kubernetes, managing a fleet of microservices becomes seamless, with features like automatic scaling, service discovery, and rolling updates.

Scalability is another major advantage of containerization, with containers providing a lightweight and efficient means of scaling applications based on demand. With container orchestration platforms, developers can define scaling policies and let the platform handle the provisioning and scaling of containers automatically. CLI commands like **kubectl scale** enable developers to scale their applications horizontally, adding or removing container instances dynamically to match workload fluctuations.

Containerization fosters consistency and reproducibility in software deployments, ensuring that applications behave consistently across different environments, from development to production. By packaging applications and dependencies into containers, developers can avoid dependency conflicts and configuration drift, leading to more reliable and predictable deployments. CLI commands like **docker push** and **docker pull** facilitate the distribution of container images across different environments, enabling seamless deployment workflows.

Security is a critical concern in software development, and containerization offers several mechanisms to enhance application security. Containers provide isolation at the application level, reducing the attack surface and limiting the impact of security vulnerabilities. Features like container image scanning and runtime security policies help identify and mitigate security risks. CLI commands like **docker scan** allow developers to scan container images for known vulnerabilities before deploying them to production environments, ensuring a secure software supply chain.

Resource efficiency is another compelling benefit of containerization, with containers sharing the host operating system's kernel and utilizing resources more efficiently compared to virtual machines. Containers start up quickly, have minimal overhead, and can be packed densely on a host, optimizing resource utilization and reducing infrastructure costs. CLI commands like **docker stats** provide real-time insights into container resource usage, enabling developers to optimize container configurations for performance and efficiency.

DevOps practices thrive in containerized environments, with containers bridging the gap between development and operations teams. By adopting a "container-first" approach, organizations can create consistent environments across the development lifecycle, from local development to testing and production. CI/CD pipelines integrate seamlessly with containerization, enabling automated testing, deployment, and rollback of containerized applications. CLI commands like **docker-compose up** facilitate local development environments, allowing developers to spin up multi-container applications with a single command.

Portability is a fundamental advantage of containerization, with containers running consistently across different infrastructure environments, including on-premises data centers, public clouds, and hybrid cloud environments. Container images, built once and run anywhere, enable organizations to embrace hybrid and multi-cloud strategies, avoiding vendor lock-in and maximizing flexibility. CLI commands like **docker save** and **docker load** facilitate the export and import of container images, enabling seamless migration of workloads across environments.

In summary, the benefits of containerization are wide-ranging and transformative, empowering organizations to develop, deploy, and scale applications with unprecedented speed, efficiency, and reliability. From fostering microservices architectures to enhancing security, scalability, and resource efficiency, containerization has become a cornerstone of modern software development and deployment practices. With containerization, organizations can innovate faster, deliver value to customers more effectively, and stay ahead in today's rapidly evolving digital landscape.

Chapter 2: Understanding Docker Fundamentals

Docker Components are essential building blocks of the Docker ecosystem, facilitating the creation, management, and deployment of containerized applications. At the core of Docker is the Docker Engine, a lightweight runtime and packaging tool for containers. The Docker Engine consists of several components, including the Docker daemon, CLI (Command Line Interface), and REST API. The Docker daemon, **dockerd**, is responsible for managing containers, images, volumes, and networks on a host system. Developers interact with the Docker daemon through the Docker CLI, issuing commands like **docker run**, **docker build**, and **docker push** to perform various container operations. The Docker REST API provides programmatic access to Docker's functionality, enabling automation and integration with other tools and systems. To start the Docker daemon, one can use the **dockerd** command, optionally specifying configuration options such as network settings and storage drivers.

Apart from the Docker Engine, other key Docker components include Docker Images, Docker Containers, Docker Registries, and Docker Volumes. Docker Images serve as the blueprints for containers, containing everything needed to run an application, including the code, runtime, libraries, and dependencies. Images are typically built from a Dockerfile, a text file that specifies the steps needed to create the image. The **docker build** command is used to build an image from a Dockerfile, while **docker pull** retrieves an image from a registry. Once an image is built or pulled, it can be instantiated as a container using the **docker run** command, specifying options such as ports, volumes, and environment variables.

Docker Containers are lightweight, isolated execution environments created from Docker images. Each container runs as a separate process on the host system, with its own filesystem, network, and process space. Containers are ephemeral by nature, meaning they can be easily started, stopped, and deleted without affecting the host system. The **docker ps** command lists the running containers on a host, while **docker stop** and **docker rm** are used to stop and remove containers, respectively. Docker Registries are repositories for storing and distributing Docker images. The Docker Hub is the official public registry maintained by Docker, hosting millions of public images that can be freely accessed and used by the community. Organizations often deploy private Docker registries for storing proprietary or sensitive images. The **docker push** and **docker pull** commands are used to upload and download images to and from a registry, respectively.

Docker Volumes provide persistent storage for containers, allowing data to survive container restarts and deletions. Volumes are used to store application data, configuration files, and other stateful information outside the container filesystem. Docker supports various types of volumes, including host-mounted volumes, named volumes, and anonymous volumes. Host-mounted volumes map a directory on the host system to a directory in the container, providing direct access to the host filesystem. Named volumes are managed by Docker and persist data independently of the container lifecycle. Anonymous volumes are temporary volumes created and managed by Docker, typically used for temporary storage. The **docker volume create**, **docker volume ls**, and **docker volume rm** commands are used to manage Docker volumes.

In addition to these core components, Docker also provides several auxiliary tools and services to enhance the Docker experience. Docker Compose is a tool for defining and running multi-container Docker applications using a simple YAML configuration file. Compose allows developers to define the services, networks, and volumes for an application in a single file, simplifying the deployment process. The **docker-compose up** command is used to start the application defined in the **docker-compose.yml** file, while **docker-compose down** stops and removes the application containers. Docker Swarm is a native clustering and orchestration tool for Docker, allowing developers to deploy and manage a cluster of Docker hosts as a single virtual host. Swarm enables features such as service discovery, load balancing, and rolling updates, making it easy to scale and manage containerized applications. The **docker swarm init** command initializes a Swarm cluster on a host, while **docker service create** deploys a service to the cluster.

In summary, Docker Components form the foundation of the Docker platform, enabling developers to build, ship, and run containerized applications with ease. From the Docker Engine and Docker Images to Docker Containers, Registries, and Volumes, each component plays a crucial role in the container lifecycle. With Docker's comprehensive set of tools and services, developers can leverage the power of containers to streamline their development workflows, improve application portability, and accelerate the delivery of software.

Key Docker Concepts encompass fundamental principles and elements essential to understanding and effectively utilizing Docker technology. At the heart of Docker lies the concept of containerization, a lightweight form of virtualization that encapsulates applications and their dependencies into self-contained units called containers. Containers enable developers to package their applications along with all the necessary libraries and dependencies, ensuring consistency and portability across different environments. The docker run command is used to create and start a container from a Docker image, specifying options such as port bindings, volume mounts, and environment variables. Docker Images serve as the blueprints for containers, providing a read-only template that contains the application code, runtime, libraries, and other dependencies. Images are built from Dockerfiles, text files that define the steps needed to create the image. The docker build command is used to build an image from a Dockerfile, while docker push uploads the image to a registry, making it available for distribution. Docker Registries are repositories for storing and sharing Docker images, allowing developers to collaborate and distribute their applications. The Docker Hub is the official public registry maintained by Docker, hosting millions of public images that can be freely accessed and used by the community. Organizations often deploy private registries to store proprietary or sensitive images. The docker pull command is used to download an image from a registry, while docker push uploads an image to a registry. Docker Containers are instances of Docker images, running as isolated processes on a host system. Each container has its own filesystem, network, and process space, providing lightweight and efficient isolation. Containers are ephemeral by nature, meaning they can be easily started, stopped, and deleted without affecting the host system. The docker ps command lists the running containers on a host, while docker stop and docker rm are used to stop and remove containers, respectively. Docker Volumes provide persistent storage for containers, allowing data to survive container restarts and deletions. Volumes are used to store application data, configuration files, and other stateful information outside the container filesystem. Docker supports various types of volumes, including host-mounted volumes, named volumes, and anonymous volumes. The docker volume create, docker volume ls, and docker volume rm commands are used to manage Docker volumes. Docker Networking enables communication between containers running on the same host or across different hosts. By default, Docker creates a bridge network for containers on a host, allowing them to communicate with each other. Developers can create custom networks using the docker network create command, specifying options such as subnet range and driver type. Docker Compose is a tool for defining and running multi-container Docker applications using a simple YAML configuration file. Compose allows developers to define the services, networks, and volumes for an application in a single file, simplifying the deployment process. The docker-compose up command is used to start the application defined in the docker-compose.yml file, while docker-compose down stops and removes the application containers. These key Docker concepts form the foundation of Docker technology, empowering developers to build, ship, and run containerized applications with ease and efficiency.

Chapter 3: Installing Docker on Your System

Supported Platforms for Docker encompass a wide array of operating systems and environments, enabling developers to leverage Docker technology across diverse infrastructure setups. Docker provides official support for several major platforms, including Linux, Windows, and macOS, catering to the needs of developers working on different operating systems. Linux is the native platform for Docker, offering robust support and seamless integration with Docker's core functionalities. Docker Engine runs natively on Linux, leveraging features such as namespaces, cgroups, and the Linux kernel's capabilities to provide lightweight containerization. The **docker** command-line interface (CLI) is used to interact with Docker on Linux systems, enabling developers to manage containers, images, volumes, and networks. Windows is another supported platform for Docker, with Docker Desktop providing a user-friendly experience for developers working on Windows-based machines. Docker Desktop for Windows includes Docker Engine, Docker CLI, and Docker Compose, allowing developers to build, run, and orchestrate containers on their Windows systems. The **docker** CLI commands work similarly on Windows as they do on Linux, enabling developers to perform container operations with ease. Docker

Desktop for Windows also integrates with Hyper-V or WSL 2 (Windows Subsystem for Linux 2) for running Linux containers on Windows, providing flexibility and interoperability. macOS is also a supported platform for Docker development, with Docker Desktop for Mac offering a seamless experience for developers working on Apple hardware. Docker Desktop for Mac includes Docker Engine, Docker CLI, and Docker Compose, allowing developers to build, run, and orchestrate containers on their macOS systems. Under the hood, Docker Desktop for Mac leverages HyperKit, a lightweight hypervisor built on top of macOS's Hypervisor.framework, to run Linux containers on macOS. The **docker** CLI commands can be used on macOS to manage containers, images, volumes, and networks, providing a consistent experience across different platforms. In addition to these major platforms, Docker also provides support for other environments, such as cloud platforms and virtualized infrastructure. Docker Engine can be installed on various cloud platforms, including Amazon Web Services (AWS), Microsoft Azure, and Google Cloud Platform (GCP), allowing developers to deploy and manage containers in the cloud. The **docker-machine** command-line tool can be used to provision Docker hosts on cloud platforms, enabling developers to create and manage Docker Swarm clusters for container orchestration. Docker also supports virtualized environments, such as VMware, VirtualBox, and Vagrant, allowing developers to run

Docker containers on virtual machines for development and testing purposes. By supporting a wide range of platforms, Docker enables developers to build, ship, and run containerized applications across different environments, providing flexibility and interoperability. Whether developers are working on Linux, Windows, macOS, or cloud platforms, Docker offers a consistent and unified experience for container development and deployment.

Installation Steps for Docker are crucial for getting started with containerization and leveraging Docker technology for developing and deploying applications. Docker provides straightforward installation procedures for various operating systems and environments, ensuring that developers can quickly set up Docker on their systems and start building containers. The installation steps vary depending on the platform, but Docker offers comprehensive documentation and installation guides for each supported environment.
For Linux-based systems, Docker offers two editions: Docker Engine - Community and Docker Engine - Enterprise. The installation process for Docker on Linux typically involves adding the Docker repository to the system's package manager, installing the Docker package, and starting the Docker service. On Debian-based distributions such as Ubuntu, the installation process involves running commands like **sudo apt-get update** to update the package index,

followed by **sudo apt-get install docker-ce docker-ce-cli containerd.io** to install Docker. After installation, the Docker service can be started and enabled to run on system boot using commands like **sudo systemctl start docker** and **sudo systemctl enable docker**.

For Windows-based systems, Docker Desktop provides an intuitive installation experience, allowing developers to install Docker Engine, Docker CLI, and Docker Compose on their Windows machines. The installation package for Docker Desktop can be downloaded from the Docker website and executed to start the installation process. During installation, Docker Desktop sets up the necessary components, including Hyper-V or WSL 2 for running Linux containers on Windows. Once installed, Docker Desktop can be launched from the Start menu, providing developers with a Docker CLI terminal and a system tray icon for easy access to Docker-related tasks.

On macOS, Docker Desktop offers a seamless installation process, enabling developers to run Docker containers on their Apple hardware. The installation package for Docker Desktop can be downloaded from the Docker website and dragged into the Applications folder to install Docker. Docker Desktop for Mac includes Docker Engine, Docker CLI, and Docker Compose, providing a complete Docker development environment on macOS. Once installed, Docker Desktop can be launched from the

Applications folder, allowing developers to manage Docker containers and images using the Docker CLI.

In addition to these desktop platforms, Docker also provides installation options for cloud environments, virtual machines, and server setups. On cloud platforms like AWS, Azure, and GCP, Docker Engine can be deployed using cloud-specific tools and services, such as AWS CloudFormation templates, Azure Resource Manager templates, or GCP Deployment Manager templates. For virtualized environments, Docker supports integration with hypervisors like VMware, VirtualBox, and Hyper-V, enabling developers to run Docker containers on virtual machines. Docker also offers installation guides for server setups, including standalone installations and clustered deployments using Docker Swarm or Kubernetes.

Overall, the installation steps for Docker are straightforward and well-documented, allowing developers to set up Docker on their preferred platforms quickly. By following the installation guides provided by Docker, developers can create a robust containerization environment and start building, shipping, and running containerized applications with ease. Whether on Linux, Windows, macOS, or in the cloud, Docker provides a consistent and unified experience for container development and deployment.

Chapter 4: Docker Containers vs. Virtual Machines

Comparison of Virtualization Technologies involves assessing the strengths, weaknesses, and use cases of various virtualization solutions to determine the most suitable option for specific scenarios. Virtualization technologies enable the creation of virtualized environments, allowing multiple operating systems and applications to run on a single physical hardware platform. Two prominent virtualization technologies are traditional hypervisor-based virtualization and containerization, each offering distinct advantages and trade-offs.

Hypervisor-based virtualization, exemplified by platforms like VMware vSphere and Microsoft Hyper-V, involves the abstraction of physical hardware resources into virtual machines (VMs), each running its own guest operating system. Hypervisors, such as VMware ESXi and Microsoft Hyper-V, sit directly on the physical hardware and manage the allocation of CPU, memory, storage, and networking resources to VMs. The hypervisor provides isolation between VMs, ensuring that each VM operates independently of others, with its own kernel and system libraries.

The installation of a hypervisor typically involves downloading the hypervisor software, creating a bootable installation media, and booting the host system from the installation media. Once installed, administrators can manage the hypervisor and create VMs using management tools provided by the hypervisor vendor. CLI commands such as **esxcli** for VMware ESXi and **Hyper-V PowerShell cmdlets** for Microsoft Hyper-V are commonly used to perform tasks such as creating VMs, configuring virtual networks, and managing storage resources.

Containerization, on the other hand, is a lightweight form of virtualization that abstracts applications and their dependencies into isolated units called containers. Containers share the host operating system's kernel and resources, enabling efficient resource utilization and rapid application deployment. Docker is the most popular containerization platform, providing tools for creating, deploying, and managing containers.

To deploy applications in containers, developers typically start by creating a Dockerfile, a text file that defines the steps needed to build a container image. Commands like **docker build** are then used to build the image from the Dockerfile, and **docker run** is used to instantiate the container from the image. Docker Engine, the runtime engine for containers, runs on various operating systems, including Linux, Windows, and macOS, providing a consistent experience for container deployment across different platforms.

One key difference between hypervisor-based virtualization and containerization is the level of overhead and performance impact. Hypervisor-based virtualization imposes a higher overhead due to the need to run multiple guest operating systems, each with its own kernel, system libraries, and device drivers. This overhead can lead to increased resource consumption and reduced performance compared to containerization. Containers, on the other hand, are lightweight and share the host operating system's kernel, resulting in minimal overhead and near-native performance for containerized applications.

Another difference lies in the level of isolation provided by each technology. Hypervisor-based virtualization provides strong isolation between VMs, with each VM running its own kernel and system stack. This level of isolation makes hypervisor-based virtualization well-suited for scenarios requiring strict security and multi-tenancy, such as hosting providers and data centers. Containers, while providing isolation at the application level, share the same kernel and system libraries, leading to a lower degree of isolation compared to VMs.

The choice between hypervisor-based virtualization and containerization depends on various factors, including performance requirements, resource utilization, security considerations, and application architecture. For scenarios where strong isolation and compatibility with legacy applications are paramount, hypervisor-based virtualization may be the preferred option. Conversely, for environments requiring lightweight, agile, and scalable deployment of modern microservices-based applications, containerization offers significant advantages in terms of performance, resource efficiency, and agility.

In summary, the comparison of virtualization technologies involves evaluating the trade-offs between hypervisor-based virtualization and containerization to determine the most suitable solution for specific use cases. While hypervisor-based virtualization offers strong isolation and compatibility with legacy applications, containerization provides lightweight, efficient, and scalable deployment options for modern cloud-native applications. By understanding the characteristics and capabilities of each technology, organizations can make informed decisions about their virtualization strategies and optimize their infrastructure for performance, agility, and cost-effectiveness.

Advantages of Docker Containers are manifold, revolutionizing the landscape of software development and deployment. Docker containers offer a lightweight, portable, and efficient approach to packaging and running applications, providing numerous benefits to developers, IT operations teams, and organizations as a whole.

One of the key advantages of Docker containers is their consistency across different environments, ensuring that applications behave the same way regardless of the underlying infrastructure. Docker containers encapsulate all the dependencies, libraries, and configuration settings needed to run an application, eliminating the "it works on my machine" problem often encountered in traditional development environments.

To create a Docker container, developers start by defining a Dockerfile, a text file that specifies the steps needed to build the container image. Commands like **docker build** are then used to build the image from the Dockerfile, ensuring that the containerized application is built consistently every time, regardless of the developer's environment. Once built, the same container image can be deployed to any environment that supports Docker, whether it's a developer's laptop, a testing server, or a production cluster.

Another advantage of Docker containers is their lightweight nature, enabling efficient resource utilization and rapid deployment of applications. Unlike traditional virtual machines, which require a separate operating system kernel for each instance, Docker containers share the host operating system's kernel, resulting in minimal overhead and faster startup times.

The **docker run** command is used to instantiate a Docker container from an image, specifying options such as CPU and memory limits, network settings, and environment variables. Containers start up almost instantaneously, making them ideal for dynamic and scalable environments where applications need to be spun up and down quickly in response to changing demand.

Scalability is another key advantage of Docker containers, with Docker providing built-in support for horizontal scaling and load balancing. By leveraging container orchestration platforms like Kubernetes or Docker Swarm, organizations can deploy and manage fleets of containers across clusters of hosts, automatically scaling applications based on resource utilization and incoming traffic.

With Docker containers, organizations can embrace microservices architecture, breaking down monolithic applications into smaller, decoupled components that can be developed, deployed, and scaled independently. Each microservice runs in its own container, enabling teams to iterate on and release features more rapidly without impacting other parts of the application.

The **docker-compose** command-line tool simplifies the management of multi-container applications, allowing developers to define services, networks, and volumes in a single YAML configuration file. With Docker Compose, developers can spin up entire application stacks with a single command, streamlining the development and testing process.

Security is a critical concern in software development, and Docker containers offer several features to enhance application security. Containers provide process isolation, ensuring that each container runs in its own namespace with limited access to system resources. Docker also supports user namespaces, allowing containers to run with reduced privileges, further reducing the risk of security breaches.

Docker provides features like image signing and content trust, enabling organizations to verify the integrity and authenticity of container images before deployment. By signing container images with cryptographic keys, organizations can ensure that only trusted images are allowed to run in their environments, mitigating the risk of running malicious or tampered images.

Portability is another significant advantage of Docker containers, allowing applications to run consistently across different infrastructure environments, including on-premises data centers, public clouds, and hybrid cloud setups. Docker images are platform-independent, meaning that the same image can be deployed to any environment that supports Docker, regardless of the underlying infrastructure or operating system.

By leveraging Docker containers, organizations can accelerate their software development lifecycle, improve resource utilization, enhance security, and achieve greater flexibility and portability in their applications. Whether developing cloud-native microservices, deploying legacy applications, or orchestrating containerized workloads at scale, Docker containers offer a powerful and versatile solution for modern software development and deployment.

Chapter 5: Managing Docker Images

Pulling Images from Docker Hub is a fundamental aspect of Docker container management, providing developers with access to a vast repository of container images that can be used as building blocks for their applications. Docker Hub serves as the official public registry for Docker images, hosting millions of pre-built images contributed by the community and curated by Docker. Pulling images from Docker Hub is a straightforward process that involves using the **docker pull** command to download the desired image to the local system.

To pull an image from Docker Hub, developers start by identifying the name and tag of the image they want to download. Images on Docker Hub are typically named in the format **<repository>/<image>:<tag>**, where the repository represents the user or organization that owns the image, the image is the name of the image, and the tag specifies a specific version or variant of the image. For example, the official Nginx image on Docker Hub is named **nginx**, and it has multiple tags representing different versions, such as **latest**, **alpine**, and **1.19**.

To pull the latest version of the Nginx image from Docker Hub, developers can use the **docker pull** command followed by the image name:

Copy code

```
docker pull nginx
```

This command instructs the Docker daemon to download the latest version of the Nginx image from Docker Hub and store it locally on the system. If the image with the specified name does not exist on the local system, Docker will initiate the download process, fetching the image layers from Docker Hub and assembling them into a complete image.
Developers can also specify a specific tag when pulling an image from Docker Hub to download a particular version or variant of the image. For example, to pull the Nginx image tagged as **alpine**, developers can use the following command:
Copy code

```
docker pull nginx:alpine
```

This command instructs Docker to download the Nginx image with the **alpine** tag, which is a lightweight variant of the Nginx image based on the Alpine Linux distribution. Using specific tags allows developers to ensure consistency and reproducibility in their container environments by pulling a specific version of an image.
In addition to pulling images by name and tag, developers can also specify the full image URL when pulling images from Docker Hub. This is useful when pulling images from repositories other than the official library or when using private repositories hosted on Docker Hub or other registries.
For example, to pull an image named **myapp** from a private repository on Docker Hub, developers can use the following command:
bashCopy code

```
docker pull myusername/myapp
```

This command instructs Docker to pull the **myapp** image from the repository owned by **myusername** on Docker Hub. If the repository requires authentication, Docker will prompt the user to enter their Docker Hub credentials before initiating the pull operation.

Pulling images from Docker Hub is a crucial step in the containerization process, enabling developers to access a wide range of pre-built images for use in their applications. By leveraging Docker Hub's extensive library of images, developers can streamline their development workflows, reduce duplication of effort, and accelerate the deployment of containerized applications. Whether pulling official images from the Docker library or custom images from private repositories, Docker Hub provides a centralized platform for sharing and distributing container images, fostering collaboration and innovation within the Docker community.

Building Custom Images is a fundamental aspect of Docker containerization, enabling developers to create tailored environments for their applications by defining custom configurations, installing dependencies, and packaging application code into container images. Docker provides a powerful and flexible mechanism for building custom images using Dockerfiles, text files that specify the steps needed to build the image. Dockerfiles use a simple and intuitive syntax to describe the image's contents, making it easy for developers to automate the image creation process and ensure reproducibility across different environments.

To build a custom image, developers start by creating a Dockerfile in the root directory of their application code. The Dockerfile contains a series of instructions, each corresponding to a step in the image-building process.

One of the first steps in a Dockerfile is typically to specify the base image upon which the custom image will be built. The base image provides the foundation for the custom image, including the operating system, runtime environment, and system libraries.

For example, to build an image for a Node.js application, developers can use the official Node.js base image, which provides a pre-configured environment for running Node.js applications.

The **FROM** instruction is used in the Dockerfile to specify the base image:

cssCopy code

```
FROM node:14
```

This instruction tells Docker to use the Node.js 14 base image as the starting point for building the custom image. Docker will automatically pull the specified base image from Docker Hub if it is not already available locally.

Once the base image is defined, developers can use additional instructions in the Dockerfile to customize the image according to their requirements. This may include installing system packages and dependencies, copying application code into the image, setting environment variables, and defining container runtime settings.

For example, to copy the application code into the image and set the working directory, developers can use the **COPY** and **WORKDIR** instructions:

bashCopy code

```
COPY . /app WORKDIR /app
```

These instructions tell Docker to copy all files and directories from the current directory on the host system into the **/app** directory in the image, and then set **/app** as the working directory for subsequent commands.

After defining the image's contents and configurations in the Dockerfile, developers can use the **docker build** command to build the custom image. The **docker build** command takes the path to the directory containing the Dockerfile as an argument and initiates the image-building process.

For example, to build the custom image using the Dockerfile located in the current directory, developers can use the following command:

Copy code

```
docker build -t myapp .
```

This command instructs Docker to build the image using the Dockerfile in the current directory (**.**) and tag the resulting image with the name **myapp**. Docker will execute each instruction in the Dockerfile sequentially, creating intermediate container layers and caching the results to improve build performance.

During the build process, developers can monitor the progress and view the output of each instruction as Docker executes them. If an instruction fails, Docker will abort the build process and display an error message, allowing developers to identify and troubleshoot issues. Once the build process is complete, developers can use the **docker images** command to view the list of available images on their system, including the newly built custom image.

Copy code

```
docker images
```

This command lists all images stored locally on the system, including the image tagged as **myapp** that was built in the previous step. Developers can then use the custom image to run containers, deploy applications, and share with others.

Building custom images with Docker provides developers with a powerful tool for creating consistent and reproducible environments for their applications. By defining custom configurations, installing dependencies, and packaging application code into container images, developers can streamline the deployment process, improve collaboration, and ensure that applications run consistently across different environments. With Docker's intuitive and flexible image-building process, developers can easily automate the creation of custom images and integrate them into their development workflows, accelerating the delivery of containerized applications.

Chapter 6: Running Your First Docker Container

Basic Docker Commands are essential tools for managing containers, images, volumes, networks, and other Docker resources in a Dockerized environment. These commands provide developers, system administrators, and DevOps engineers with the necessary tools to build, run, and manage containerized applications effectively.

One of the most fundamental Docker commands is **docker run**, which is used to create and start containers based on Docker images. To run a container, developers specify the image name along with any desired options, such as port mappings, volume mounts, and environment variables. For example, to run a container based on the official Nginx image in detached mode (background), exposing port 80 on the host system, the following command can be used:

arduinoCopy code

```
docker run -d -p 80:80 nginx
```

This command tells Docker to create and start a container based on the **nginx** image, running it in detached mode (**-d**) and mapping port 80 on the host system to port 80 in the container (**-p 80:80**).

To list the running containers on a Docker host, developers can use the **docker ps** command:

Copy code

docker ps

This command displays a list of running containers along with relevant information such as container ID, image name, status, and exposed ports. If developers want to see all containers, including those that are stopped, they can use the **-a** flag:

cssCopy code

docker ps -a

To stop a running container, developers can use the **docker stop** command followed by the container ID or name:

arduinoCopy code

docker stop <container_id or container_name>

Similarly, to remove a container from the system, the **docker rm** command can be used:

bashCopy code

docker rm <container_id or container_name>

To inspect detailed information about a container, including its configuration, network settings, and resource usage, developers can use the **docker inspect** command followed by the container ID or name:

phpCopy code

docker inspect <container_id or container_name>

Another essential Docker command is **docker pull**, which is used to download Docker images from Docker Hub or other container registries. To pull an image from Docker Hub, developers specify the image name along with an optional tag:

phpCopy code

```
docker pull <image_name:tag>
```

For example, to pull the latest version of the Ubuntu image from Docker Hub, developers can use the following command:

Copy code

```
docker pull ubuntu
```

To list all available Docker images stored locally on the system, developers can use the **docker images** command:

Copy code

```
docker images
```

This command displays a list of images along with information such as repository, tag, image ID, and size.

To remove a Docker image from the local system, developers can use the **docker rmi** command followed by the image ID or name:

phpCopy code

```
docker rmi <image_id or image_name>
```

Docker also provides commands for managing volumes, which are used to persist data generated by containers. To create a volume, developers can use the **docker volume create** command followed by the volume name:

luaCopy code

```
docker volume create <volume_name>
```

To list all volumes on the system, developers can use the **docker volume ls** command:

bashCopy code

```
docker volume ls
```

To remove a volume from the system, developers can use the **docker volume rm** command followed by the volume name or ID:

bashCopy code

```
docker volume rm <volume_name or volume_id>
```

In addition to managing containers, images, and volumes, Docker also provides commands for managing networks, configuring Docker Engine settings, and interacting with Docker registries.

Overall, basic Docker commands are essential tools for anyone working with Docker containers, providing a convenient and efficient way to build, run, and manage containerized applications. By mastering these commands, developers and system administrators can effectively leverage Docker's powerful features to streamline their workflows, improve collaboration, and enhance the deployment of containerized applications.

Interacting with Containers is a fundamental aspect of working with Docker, allowing developers, system administrators, and DevOps engineers to manage and troubleshoot containerized applications effectively. Docker provides a rich set of command-line interface (CLI) tools for interacting with containers, enabling users to perform various tasks such as starting, stopping, inspecting, and managing the lifecycle of containers.

One of the most basic commands for interacting with containers is **docker ps**, which is used to list the running containers on a Docker host. By running this command without any options, users can view a list of active containers along with essential information such as container ID, image name, status, and exposed ports.

Copy code

```
docker ps
```

If users want to see all containers, including those that are stopped, they can add the **-a** flag to the command:

cssCopy code

```
docker ps -a
```

To start a stopped container, users can use the **docker start** command followed by the container ID or name:

phpCopy code

```
docker start <container_id or container_name>
```

Conversely, to stop a running container, users can use the **docker stop** command followed by the container ID or name:

arduinoCopy code

```
docker stop <container_id or container_name>
```

To restart a container, users can combine the **docker stop** and **docker start** commands into a single command:

phpCopy code

```
docker restart <container_id or container_name>
```

Users can also remove stopped containers from the system using the **docker rm** command followed by the container ID or name:

bashCopy code

```
docker rm <container_id or container_name>
```

To inspect detailed information about a container, including its configuration, network settings, and resource usage, users can use the **docker inspect** command followed by the container ID or name:

phpCopy code

```
docker inspect <container_id or container_name>
```

This command provides a comprehensive JSON output containing information about the specified container.

Another essential command for interacting with containers is **docker exec**, which is used to execute commands inside a running container. Users can specify the container ID or name along with the desired command to execute within the container's environment.

bashCopy code

```
docker exec <container_id or container_name> <command>
```

For example, to execute a bash shell inside a running container named **my_container**, users can use the following command:

bashCopy code

```
docker exec -it my_container bash
```

This command starts an interactive bash session within the specified container, allowing users to run commands and interact with the container's filesystem and environment.

To attach to a running container's console and interact with its primary process, users can use the **docker attach** command followed by the container ID or name:

arduinoCopy code

```
docker attach <container_id or container_name>
```

This command attaches the user's terminal to the standard input, output, and error streams of the specified container, allowing them to interact with the container's main process directly.

In addition to these basic commands, Docker provides a range of other commands and options for interacting with containers, including managing container networks, volumes, logs, and environment variables. By mastering these commands, users can effectively manage and troubleshoot containerized applications, ensuring smooth operation and optimal performance in Docker environments.

Chapter 7: Networking in Docker

Overview of Docker Networking is crucial for understanding how containers communicate with each other and with external networks in Docker environments. Docker provides a robust networking model that enables seamless communication between containers running on the same host or across different hosts in a distributed environment. Docker networking allows containers to connect to each other, share data, and access external resources such as the internet and other services.
One of the key concepts in Docker networking is the Docker network, which provides an isolated communication space for containers. Docker supports various network drivers, each offering different capabilities and features to meet different use cases. The default network driver used by Docker is the bridge network driver, which creates an internal network bridge on the Docker host, allowing containers to communicate with each other over this bridge.
To list the available Docker networks on a host, users can use the **docker network ls** command:
bashCopy code
```
docker network ls
```
This command displays a list of all Docker networks on the system, along with their names, driver types, and other relevant information.

Users can create a new Docker network using the **docker network create** command followed by the desired network name and options:

luaCopy code

```
docker network create my_network
```

This command creates a new Docker network named **my_network** using the default bridge network driver. Users can specify additional options such as the network subnet, gateway, and IP address range to customize the network configuration according to their requirements.

Once a Docker network is created, users can connect containers to the network using the **docker network connect** command followed by the network name and the container ID or name:

arduinoCopy code

```
docker network connect my_network my_container
```

This command attaches the specified container (**my_container**) to the **my_network** network, allowing it to communicate with other containers connected to the same network.

Conversely, users can disconnect containers from a network using the **docker network disconnect** command followed by the network name and the container ID or name:

arduinoCopy code

```
docker network disconnect my_network my_container
```

This command removes the specified container (**my_container**) from the **my_network** network, preventing it from communicating with other containers on the network.

In addition to the bridge network driver, Docker also supports other network drivers such as overlay, macvlan, and host, each offering specific features and capabilities for different networking scenarios.

The overlay network driver, for example, enables multi-host networking for containerized applications deployed across multiple Docker hosts. To create an overlay network, users can use the **docker network create** command with the **--driver overlay** option:

luaCopy code

```
docker network create --driver overlay my_overlay_network
```

This command creates a new overlay network named **my_overlay_network** that spans multiple Docker hosts, allowing containers to communicate with each other across hosts.

The macvlan network driver, on the other hand, enables containers to have their own MAC addresses and appear as physical devices on the network. To create a macvlan network, users can use the **docker network create** command with the **--driver macvlan** option:

cssCopy code

```
docker network create --driver macvlan --subnet=192.168.1.0/24 --gateway=192.168.1.1 -o parent=eth0 my_macvlan_network
```

This command creates a new macvlan network named **my_macvlan_network** with the specified subnet, gateway, and parent interface (**eth0**).

The host network driver, meanwhile, allows containers to share the network namespace with the Docker host, enabling them to bypass Docker's network isolation and interact directly with the host's network interfaces. To use the host network driver, users can specify the **--network=host** option when running a container:

arduinoCopy code

```
docker run --network=host my_container
```

This command runs a container named **my_container** using the host network mode, allowing it to access the host's network interfaces directly.

Overall, Docker networking provides a flexible and powerful way to connect containers and enable communication between them in Docker environments. By understanding the various network drivers and their capabilities, users can design and deploy containerized applications that meet their networking requirements and ensure seamless communication between containers running in Docker environments.

Configuring Container Networks is an essential aspect

of managing Docker environments, allowing users to define custom network settings for containers to meet specific networking requirements. Docker provides a range of options for configuring container networks, including specifying network drivers, customizing IP addressing, setting up network aliases, and defining network policies.

One of the first steps in configuring container networks is choosing the appropriate network driver. Docker supports multiple network drivers, each offering different features and capabilities to suit various networking scenarios. The default network driver used by Docker is the bridge network driver, which creates an internal network bridge on the Docker host, allowing containers to communicate with each other over this bridge.

To create a bridge network for containers, users can use the **docker network create** command followed by the desired network name and options:

luaCopy code

```
docker network create my_bridge_network
```

This command creates a new bridge network named **my_bridge_network** using the default bridge network driver.

Users can also specify additional options such as the subnet, gateway, and IP address range when creating a bridge network to customize the network configuration according to their requirements:

cssCopy code

docker network create --subnet=192.168.0.0/16 --gateway=192.168.0.1 my_bridge_network

This command creates a new bridge network named **my_bridge_network** with the specified subnet (**192.168.0.0/16**) and gateway (**192.168.0.1**).

Once a bridge network is created, users can connect containers to the network using the **docker run** command with the **--network** option followed by the network name:

arduinoCopy code

docker run --network=my_bridge_network my_container

This command runs a container named **my_container** and connects it to the **my_bridge_network** network.

In addition to the bridge network driver, Docker also supports other network drivers such as overlay, macvlan, and host, each offering specific features and capabilities for different networking scenarios.

The overlay network driver enables multi-host networking for containerized applications deployed across multiple Docker hosts. To create an overlay network, users can use the **docker network create** command with the **--driver overlay** option:

luaCopy code

docker network create --driver overlay my_overlay_network

This command creates a new overlay network named **my_overlay_network** that spans multiple Docker hosts, allowing containers to communicate with each other across hosts.

The macvlan network driver enables containers to have their own MAC addresses and appear as physical devices on the network. To create a macvlan network, users can use the **docker network create** command with the **--driver macvlan** option:

cssCopy code

```
docker network create --driver macvlan --subnet=192.168.1.0/24 --gateway=192.168.1.1 -o parent=eth0 my_macvlan_network
```

This command creates a new macvlan network named **my_macvlan_network** with the specified subnet, gateway, and parent interface (**eth0**).

The host network driver allows containers to share the network namespace with the Docker host, enabling them to bypass Docker's network isolation and interact directly with the host's network interfaces. To use the host network driver, users can specify the **--network=host** option when running a container:

arduinoCopy code

```
docker run --network=host my_container
```

This command runs a container named **my_container** using the host network mode, allowing it to access the host's network interfaces directly.

In addition to specifying network drivers and options, users can also configure advanced network settings such as network aliases, DNS settings, and network policies to control traffic flow and access between containers and external networks.

Overall, configuring container networks is a critical aspect of managing Docker environments effectively, enabling users to define custom network settings to meet specific requirements and ensure seamless communication between containers running in Docker environments. By understanding the available network drivers and their capabilities, users can design and deploy containerized applications with flexible and reliable networking configurations that support their business needs.

Chapter 8: Docker Volumes

Introduction to Docker Volumes is essential for understanding how to manage persistent data in Docker containers effectively. Docker volumes provide a mechanism for storing and persisting data generated by containers, ensuring that data persists even after containers are stopped or removed. Docker volumes are crucial for applications that require persistent storage, such as databases, file servers, and stateful applications.
One of the primary use cases for Docker volumes is storing application data that needs to persist across container restarts and updates. Docker volumes decouple data storage from the container lifecycle, allowing containers to be replaced or updated without losing important data.
To create a Docker volume, users can use the **docker volume create** command followed by the desired volume name:
luaCopy code

```
docker volume create my_volume
```

This command creates a new Docker volume named **my_volume** on the Docker host. Users can specify additional options such as the volume driver and driver-specific options to customize the volume configuration according to their requirements.
Once a Docker volume is created, users can mount the volume into containers using the **-v** or **--mount** option when running the container:

arduinoCopy code

```
docker run -v my_volume:/path/to/mount/point my_container
```

This command mounts the **my_volume** volume into the container at the specified mount point (**/path/to/mount/point**). Any data written to this mount point within the container is stored in the Docker volume on the host.

Users can also use named volumes to manage volumes more conveniently. Named volumes are volumes that have a specific name assigned to them, making them easier to reference and manage. To create a named volume, users can specify the volume name directly in the **-v** or **--mount** option when running the container:

arduinoCopy code

```
docker run -v my_named_volume:/path/to/mount/point my_container
```

This command creates a named volume named **my_named_volume** and mounts it into the container at the specified mount point (**/path/to/mount/point**).

In addition to creating volumes explicitly, Docker also supports anonymous volumes, which are volumes that are managed internally by Docker and do not have a specific name assigned to them. Anonymous volumes are created automatically when a container is started with a volume mounted into it, and they are typically used for temporary data storage or for sharing data between containers.

To mount an anonymous volume into a container, users can specify a mount point without specifying a volume name:

arduinoCopy code

```
docker run -v /path/to/mount/point my_container
```

This command mounts an anonymous volume into the container at the specified mount point (**/path/to/mount/point**). Docker automatically assigns a unique name to the volume and manages it internally.

Docker volumes also support various volume drivers, allowing users to use different storage backends and technologies for storing data. Docker provides several built-in volume drivers, including local, NFS, and Amazon Elastic Block Store (EBS). Users can specify the desired volume driver and driver-specific options when creating volumes or mounting volumes into containers.

To specify a volume driver when creating a volume, users can use the **--driver** option with the **docker volume create** command:

bashCopy code

```
docker volume create --driver local --opt type=ext4 --opt device=/dev/sdb my_custom_volume
```

This command creates a new Docker volume named **my_custom_volume** using the local volume driver and specifies additional driver-specific options such as the filesystem type (**ext4**) and the device to use (**/dev/sdb**).

To use a specific volume driver when mounting a volume into a container, users can specify the driver and driver-specific options in the **-v** or **--mount** option:

typescriptCopy code

```
docker run -v
my_custom_volume:/path/to/mount/point --mount
type=nfs,source=my_nfs_volume,target=/path/to/mount/point my_container
```

This command mounts the **my_custom_volume** volume using the local volume driver and mounts the **my_nfs_volume** volume using the NFS volume driver into the container at the specified mount points.

Overall, Docker volumes provide a powerful and flexible mechanism for managing persistent data in Docker containers. By understanding how to create, mount, and manage volumes, users can effectively manage data storage in Docker environments and ensure that their containerized applications have access to reliable and persistent storage solutions. Data Management with Volumes is a critical aspect of Docker containerization, enabling users to efficiently manage and persist data generated by containerized applications. Docker volumes provide a flexible and powerful solution for storing and managing data, allowing containers to access and manipulate data independently of the container lifecycle. With Docker volumes, users can ensure data persistence across container restarts, updates, and migrations, making them ideal for applications that require persistent storage, such as databases, file servers, and stateful applications. One of the primary benefits of using Docker volumes for data management is decoupling data storage from the container lifecycle. Docker volumes allow users to store data separately from containers, ensuring that data

persists even if containers are stopped, removed, or replaced. This decoupling enables users to update or replace containers without affecting the underlying data, providing greater flexibility and agility in managing containerized applications.
Creating and managing Docker volumes is straightforward using the Docker CLI. Users can create a Docker volume using the **docker volume create** command followed by the desired volume name:
luaCopy code
```
docker volume create my_volume
```
This command creates a new Docker volume named **my_volume** on the Docker host. Users can specify additional options such as the volume driver and driver-specific options to customize the volume configuration according to their requirements.
Once a Docker volume is created, users can mount the volume into containers using the **-v** or **--mount** option when running the container:
arduinoCopy code
```
docker run -v my_volume:/path/to/mount/point my_container
```
This command mounts the **my_volume** volume into the container at the specified mount point (**/path/to/mount/point**). Any data written to this mount point within the container is stored in the Docker volume on the host.
Users can also use named volumes to manage volumes more conveniently. Named volumes are volumes that have a specific name assigned to them, making them

easier to reference and manage. To create a named volume, users can specify the volume name directly in the **-v** or **--mount** option when running the container:

arduinoCopy code

```
docker run -v my_named_volume:/path/to/mount/point my_container
```

This command creates a named volume named **my_named_volume** and mounts it into the container at the specified mount point (**/path/to/mount/point**).

In addition to creating volumes explicitly, Docker also supports anonymous volumes, which are volumes that are managed internally by Docker and do not have a specific name assigned to them. Anonymous volumes are created automatically when a container is started with a volume mounted into it, and they are typically used for temporary data storage or for sharing data between containers.

To mount an anonymous volume into a container, users can specify a mount point without specifying a volume name:

arduinoCopy code

```
docker run -v /path/to/mount/point my_container
```

This command mounts an anonymous volume into the container at the specified mount point (**/path/to/mount/point**). Docker automatically assigns a unique name to the volume and manages it internally.

Once containers are running and accessing data stored in volumes, users can manage data within volumes using standard file system commands or by interacting with the containers themselves. Users can write data to volumes, read data from volumes, and manipulate data within volumes as needed to support the requirements of their containerized applications.

Overall, Docker volumes provide a robust and flexible solution for managing data in Docker environments. By leveraging Docker volumes, users can ensure data persistence, decouple data storage from the container lifecycle, and efficiently manage data generated by containerized applications. With Docker volumes, users can confidently deploy and manage containerized applications that require persistent storage, enabling them to build scalable, reliable, and resilient solutions in Docker environments.

Chapter 9: Docker Compose

Docker Compose is a tool designed to simplify the management of multi-container Docker applications, enabling users to define, manage, and deploy complex application architectures using a single configuration file. This tool streamlines the process of orchestrating Docker containers by providing a convenient way to specify services, networks, and volumes within a YAML configuration file, typically named **docker-compose.yml**. This file acts as the blueprint for the entire application, allowing users to define various components and their configurations in a structured and easily understandable format.

To begin using Docker Compose, users must first install it on their system. The installation process varies depending on the operating system, but for Unix-based systems, users can typically install Docker Compose using the following command:

bashCopy code

```
sudo curl -L "https://github.com/docker/compose/releases/download/{VERSION}/docker-compose-$(uname -s)-$(uname -m)" -o /usr/local/bin/docker-compose
```

This command downloads the Docker Compose binary and installs it in the **/usr/local/bin** directory, making it accessible from the command line.

Once Docker Compose is installed, users can start defining their multi-container applications in the

docker-compose.yml file. This file resides in the root directory of the project and contains the configuration for all the services that make up the application. Each service is defined as a separate section within the YAML file, with its own set of configuration options.

For example, let's consider a simple web application that consists of a web server and a database. The **docker-compose.yml** file for this application might look like this:

yamlCopy code

```
version: '3' services: web: image: nginx:latest ports: - "80:80" db: image: mysql:latest environment: MYSQL_ROOT_PASSWORD: password
```

In this example, the **docker-compose.yml** file defines two services: **web** and **db**. The **web** service uses the **nginx:latest** image and exposes port 80 on the host. The **db** service uses the **mysql:latest** image and sets the **MYSQL_ROOT_PASSWORD** environment variable to **password**.

Once the **docker-compose.yml** file is defined, users can deploy the Docker Compose application using the following command:

bashCopy code

```
docker-compose up
```

This command reads the **docker-compose.yml** file and creates the necessary Docker containers, networks, and volumes to deploy the application. Docker Compose automatically builds any images that are not already available locally and starts the containers in the correct order based on their dependencies.

In addition to deploying the application, Docker Compose provides commands for managing the application lifecycle. For example, users can use the following commands to control the state of the Docker Compose application:

bashCopy code

```
docker-compose start docker-compose stop docker-compose restart
```

These commands start, stop, and restart all containers in the Docker Compose application, respectively.

Furthermore, Docker Compose offers commands for managing individual services within the application, such as scaling services up or down, viewing logs, and inspecting container details. For instance, users can use the following commands to perform these tasks:

bashCopy code

```
docker-compose scale web=3 docker-compose logs web docker-compose ps
```

These commands scale the **web** service to three instances, display the logs for the **web** service, and list the running containers in the Docker Compose application, respectively.

In summary, Docker Compose is an invaluable tool for simplifying the management of multi-container Docker applications. With its straightforward YAML configuration file and intuitive CLI commands, Docker Compose empowers users to define, manage, and deploy complex application architectures with ease. By leveraging Docker Compose, users can streamline the development and deployment processes, enabling them to build scalable, reliable, and resilient containerized solutions efficiently.

Writing Compose Files is an essential skill for effectively managing multi-container Docker applications, as it allows users to define the configuration and dependencies of their application components in a structured manner using YAML syntax. Docker Compose files, typically named **docker-compose.yml**, serve as blueprints for the entire application stack, enabling users to specify services, networks, volumes, and other configuration options necessary for orchestrating the containers.

To begin writing a Compose file, users need to understand its basic structure and syntax. Each Compose file starts with a version directive that specifies the version of the Compose file format being used. This version determines which features and options are available for use in the file. For instance, the following line specifies version 3 of the Compose file format:

yamlCopy code

```
version: '3'
```

After defining the version, users can proceed to define the services that make up their application. Each service is defined as a separate block within the YAML file, with the name of the service as the key. Users can then specify various configuration options for each service, such as the Docker image to use, environment variables, ports to expose, volumes to mount, and more.

For example, consider a simple web application consisting of a web server and a database. The Compose file for this application might look like this:

yamlCopy code

```
version: '3' services: web: image: nginx:latest ports: - "80:80" db: image: mysql:latest environment: MYSQL_ROOT_PASSWORD: password
```

In this example, two services are defined: **web** and **db**. The **web** service uses the **nginx:latest** Docker image and exposes port 80 on the host machine. The **db** service uses the **mysql:latest** image and sets the **MYSQL_ROOT_PASSWORD** environment variable to **password**.

Once the services are defined, users can specify additional configuration options for the entire application, such as networks, volumes, and external dependencies. For example, users can define custom networks to isolate services or specify named volumes for persisting data.

To deploy the application defined in the Compose file, users can use the **docker-compose up** command:

bashCopy code

```
docker-compose up
```

This command reads the **docker-compose.yml** file from the current directory and creates the necessary Docker containers, networks, and volumes to deploy the application. Docker Compose automatically builds any images that are not already available locally and starts the containers in the correct order based on their dependencies.

In addition to deploying the application, Docker Compose provides commands for managing the application lifecycle and interacting with individual services. For example, users can use the following commands to control the state of the Docker Compose application:

bashCopy code

```
docker-compose start docker-compose stop docker-compose restart
```

These commands start, stop, and restart all containers in the Docker Compose application, respectively. Users can also use commands like **docker-compose logs** to view the logs of specific services or **docker-compose exec** to execute commands within a running container.

In summary, writing Compose files is a fundamental skill for managing Docker applications effectively. By understanding the structure and syntax of Compose files, users can define complex application architectures and deploy them with ease using Docker Compose. With its intuitive YAML syntax and powerful command-line interface, Docker Compose simplifies the process of orchestrating multi-container applications, enabling users to build scalable, reliable, and maintainable Docker-based solutions efficiently.

Chapter 10: Docker Best Practices and Troubleshooting

Security Best Practices are crucial for ensuring the safety and integrity of Docker containers and the applications they host, as security vulnerabilities can expose sensitive data and compromise the entire system. Docker provides various tools and practices to enhance container security, helping users mitigate risks and protect their infrastructure from potential threats. One of the fundamental security practices in Docker is to ensure that host systems are properly configured and hardened to minimize the attack surface. This includes regularly applying security patches and updates, disabling unnecessary services and ports, and implementing strong authentication and access control measures. Users can leverage Docker Security Scanning to identify and address vulnerabilities in container images before deploying them into production environments. This tool automatically scans container images for known security vulnerabilities and provides actionable insights to help users remediate issues and strengthen their security posture. To perform a security scan on a Docker image, users can use the following command:

bashCopy code

```
docker scan <image_name>
```

This command initiates a scan of the specified Docker image and provides a detailed report highlighting any identified vulnerabilities, along with recommended actions to mitigate them. Additionally, users should adhere to the principle of least privilege when defining Docker container permissions and access controls. This means restricting container capabilities and permissions to only those necessary for the application to function properly. Docker Security Profiles can be used to define fine-grained access controls for containers, limiting their capabilities and interactions with the host system. For example, users can use Docker Security Profiles to restrict container access to specific resources such as the network, file system, and system calls. To create and apply a security profile to a Docker container, users can use the following commands:

bashCopy code

```
docker security profile create <profile_name> docker
run --security-profile=<profile_name> <image_name>
```

These commands create a new security profile with the specified name and apply it to the Docker container when running it. Another important aspect of Docker security is image integrity and authenticity. Users should only use trusted Docker images from reputable sources and ensure that images are signed and verified before deployment. Docker Content Trust (DCT) can be used to enforce image signing and verification, preventing the execution of unsigned or tampered images. To enable content trust for Docker, users can use the following command:

bashCopy code

```
export DOCKER_CONTENT_TRUST=1
```

This command enables content trust for Docker, requiring all images to be signed and verified before they can be pulled or run. Additionally, users can configure Docker to use specific certificate authorities (CAs) for image verification, further enhancing security. Docker also provides built-in mechanisms for isolating containers and controlling their interactions with the host system. Users can leverage Docker Security Options such as seccomp profiles, AppArmor profiles, and user namespaces to enforce additional security controls and mitigate the impact of potential container exploits. For example, users can use Docker seccomp profiles to restrict the system calls that containers are allowed to make, reducing the risk of privilege escalation attacks. To apply a seccomp profile to a Docker container, users can use the following command:

bashCopy code

```
docker run --security-opt seccomp=<profile_name> <image_name>
```

This command applies the specified seccomp profile to the Docker container when running it, restricting the container's ability to make certain system calls. Overall, implementing security best practices is essential for safeguarding Docker containers and the applications they host against potential threats and vulnerabilities. By following these practices and leveraging Docker's built-in security features, users can enhance the security posture of their containerized environments and mitigate the risk of security breaches and data leaks.

Troubleshooting Common Issues is an essential skill for Docker administrators and developers alike, as it enables them to identify and resolve problems that may arise during the deployment and management of Docker containers. Docker provides various tools and techniques to aid in troubleshooting, allowing users to diagnose issues quickly and effectively. One of the most common issues encountered when working with Docker is container networking problems, such as containers being unable to communicate with each other or with external networks. To troubleshoot networking issues, users can use the **docker network ls** command to list all available networks and verify that the containers are connected to the correct network. Additionally, users can use the **docker network inspect** command to view detailed information about a specific network, including the IP addresses assigned to containers.

bashCopy code

```
docker network ls docker network inspect <network_name>
```

Another common issue is containers failing to start or crashing unexpectedly. To troubleshoot these issues, users can use the **docker ps** command to list all running containers and check their status. Additionally, users can use the **docker logs** command to view the logs generated by a specific container, which can provide valuable insights into the cause of the failure.

bashCopy code

```
docker ps docker logs <container_id>
```

Memory and resource constraints can also cause issues with Docker containers, such as containers being killed due to out-of-memory errors. To troubleshoot these issues, users can use the **docker stats** command to monitor resource usage for all running containers and identify any containers that may be consuming excessive resources. Additionally, users can use the **docker inspect** command to view detailed information about a specific container, including its resource limits and usage.

bashCopy code

```
docker stats docker inspect <container_id>
```

Storage-related issues, such as running out of disk space or data corruption, can also occur when working with Docker containers. To troubleshoot these issues, users can use the **docker system df** command to view disk usage information for Docker, including the amount of space used by images, containers, volumes, and other resources. Additionally, users can use the **docker volume ls** command to list all volumes and verify that they are not excessively large or consuming too much disk space.

bashCopy code

```
docker system df docker volume ls
```

Network connectivity issues, such as containers being unable to access external resources or connect to specific ports, can also occur when working with Docker containers. To troubleshoot these issues, users can use tools such as **ping**, **telnet**, or **nc** (netcat) to test network connectivity from within a container. Additionally, users can use the **docker exec** command to run diagnostic commands or tests within a running container to identify the source of the connectivity problem.

bashCopy code

```
docker exec -it <container_id> ping <hostname> docker exec -it <container_id> telnet <hostname> <port> docker exec -it <container_id> nc -v <hostname> <port>
```

Security-related issues, such as unauthorized access or compromised containers, can pose significant risks to Docker environments. To troubleshoot these issues, users can use the **docker ps** command to list all running containers and check for any unauthorized or suspicious containers. Additionally, users can use the **docker inspect** command to view detailed information about a specific container, including its security profile and settings.

bashCopy code

```
docker ps docker inspect <container_id>
```

Overall, troubleshooting common issues in Docker requires a combination of diagnostic tools, command-line utilities, and investigative techniques. By leveraging Docker's built-in tools and commands, users can quickly identify and resolve issues that may arise during the deployment and management of Docker containers, ensuring the stability and reliability of their containerized environments.

BOOK 2

MASTERING DOCKER
ADVANCED TECHNIQUES AND BEST PRACTICES

ROB BOTWRIGHT

Chapter 1: Advanced Docker Networking

Overlay Networks for Multi-Host Communication play a crucial role in facilitating communication between Docker containers deployed across multiple hosts in a distributed environment, enabling seamless connectivity and collaboration among containerized applications. Docker Swarm Mode provides built-in support for overlay networks, allowing users to create virtual networks that span multiple Docker hosts and provide transparent communication between containers regardless of their physical location. The creation of overlay networks begins with the initialization of a Docker Swarm cluster using the **docker swarm init** command, which transforms a group of Docker hosts into a single virtualized environment capable of orchestrating containers across multiple nodes.

bashCopy code

```
docker swarm init
```

Once the Swarm cluster is initialized, users can create overlay networks using the **docker network create** command, specifying the **--driver overlay** flag to indicate that the network should span multiple hosts. For example, to create an overlay network named **my-overlay-network**, users can execute the following command:

bashCopy code

```bash
docker network create --driver overlay my-overlay-network
```

This command creates a new overlay network that spans all nodes in the Docker Swarm cluster, enabling containers attached to the network to communicate with each other regardless of their physical location. Overlay networks use a distributed key-value store, such as Consul or etcd, to maintain network state and configuration across all nodes in the Swarm cluster, ensuring consistency and resilience in the face of node failures or network partitions.

To deploy containers onto an overlay network, users can use the **--network** flag when running the **docker service create** or **docker run** command. For example, to deploy a containerized web application onto the **my-overlay-network** overlay network, users can execute the following command:

bashCopy code

```bash
docker service create --name my-web-app --network my-overlay-network my-web-image
```

This command creates a new Docker service named **my-web-app** and deploys the specified container image onto the **my-overlay-network** overlay network, allowing the container to communicate with other containers on the same network regardless of their location.

Overlay networks support various features and capabilities to enhance multi-host communication and connectivity. For example, users can configure network encryption and authentication using Docker's built-in network security features, ensuring that communication between containers remains secure and private. Additionally, overlay networks support multi-tenancy and segmentation, allowing users to create separate network namespaces for different applications or teams within the same Docker Swarm cluster.

To manage overlay networks and view their configuration and status, users can use the **docker network ls**, **docker network inspect**, and **docker network rm** commands. For example, to list all overlay networks in the Docker Swarm cluster, users can execute the following command:

bashCopy code

```
docker network ls --filter driver=overlay
```

This command lists all overlay networks created with the **overlay** driver, providing information about their names, IDs, and scope. Similarly, users can inspect the configuration and status of a specific overlay network by executing the following command:

bashCopy code

```
docker network inspect my-overlay-network
```

This command displays detailed information about the **my-overlay-network** overlay network, including its subnet, gateway, and attached containers. Finally, to remove an overlay network from the Docker Swarm cluster, users can execute the following command:

bashCopy code

```
docker network rm my-overlay-network
```

This command removes the **my-overlay-network** overlay network from the Docker Swarm cluster, terminating all associated resources and releasing any allocated network resources.

In summary, overlay networks play a vital role in enabling multi-host communication and connectivity in Docker Swarm Mode, providing a scalable and resilient networking solution for distributed containerized applications. By leveraging overlay networks, users can deploy containerized applications across multiple Docker hosts with ease, ensuring seamless communication and collaboration regardless of the underlying infrastructure. With its built-in support for overlay networks, Docker Swarm Mode simplifies the deployment and management of distributed containerized applications, enabling users to build scalable and resilient microservices architectures with confidence.

Network Policies and Security are critical aspects of Docker containerization, ensuring that containerized applications are protected against unauthorized access, network threats, and data breaches. Docker provides various mechanisms and tools to implement network policies and enhance security, enabling users to define and enforce rules that govern network traffic between containers and external resources. One of the primary tools for implementing network policies in Docker is Docker Swarm Mode, which offers built-in support for network segmentation and isolation through the use of overlay networks and network ingress routing. Overlay networks enable users to create virtualized network segments that span multiple Docker hosts, allowing them to define access controls and restrictions to regulate traffic flow between containers within the same network segment.

bashCopy code

```
docker network create --driver overlay my-overlay-network
```

By creating separate overlay networks for different application components or services, users can enforce network segmentation and isolate sensitive workloads from potential threats or attacks. Additionally, Docker Swarm Mode provides network ingress routing, which enables users to define ingress rules that control external access to services running within the Swarm cluster. Users can define ingress rules using Docker service annotations or labels, specifying source IP addresses, ports, and protocols to allow or deny incoming traffic to specific services.

bashCopy code

```
docker service create --name my-web-app --network my-overlay-network --publish published=80,target=80 my-web-image
```

For example, to deploy a web application and expose it to external traffic on port 80, users can use the --

publish flag when creating the Docker service, specifying the published port and the target port on which the application is listening. This ensures that only traffic matching the specified criteria is allowed to access the service, providing an additional layer of security against unauthorized access and network-based attacks.

In addition to Docker Swarm Mode, users can implement network policies and security controls at the container level using Docker's built-in networking features and capabilities. For example, Docker allows users to define firewall rules and IP filtering using the **--iptables** flag when creating containers, enabling them to restrict incoming and outgoing network traffic based on source and destination IP addresses, ports, and protocols.

bashCopy code

```
docker run --name my-container --network my-overlay-network --iptables my-image
```

By specifying the **--iptables** flag when running a container, users can enable IP filtering and firewall rules for the container, providing granular control over network traffic and preventing unauthorized access to sensitive resources. Additionally, Docker supports network isolation and segmentation through the use of network namespaces, allowing users to create separate network namespaces for different containers or groups of containers.

bashCopy code

```
docker run --name my-container --network my-overlay-network --network-alias my-alias my-image
```

By assigning containers to specific network namespaces and using network aliases to facilitate communication between them, users can enforce network isolation and segmentation, reducing the risk of lateral movement and unauthorized access within the containerized environment. Furthermore, Docker provides network plugins and extensions that enable users to integrate third-party security solutions and tools into their Docker environments, enhancing visibility, monitoring, and enforcement capabilities.

bashCopy code

```
docker network create --driver my-security-plugin my-overlay-network
```

By leveraging network plugins and extensions, users can extend Docker's native networking capabilities and integrate advanced security features such as intrusion detection, network traffic analysis, and threat intelligence into their containerized environments. This allows users to detect and respond to security threats in real-time, ensuring the integrity and confidentiality of their containerized applications and data.

Overall, network policies and security are essential components of Docker containerization, enabling users to protect their containerized applications and infrastructure against network-based threats and attacks. By leveraging Docker's built-in networking features, tools, and extensions, users can implement robust security controls and enforce policies that regulate network traffic, prevent unauthorized access, and mitigate the risk of data breaches and security incidents. With its flexible and extensible networking architecture, Docker provides a powerful platform for implementing network security best practices and ensuring the security and compliance of containerized environments.

Chapter 2: Container Orchestration with Docker Swarm

Setting Up a Docker Swarm Cluster is a fundamental step in building a scalable and resilient container orchestration platform, enabling users to deploy and manage containerized applications across a cluster of Docker hosts. Docker Swarm is Docker's native clustering and orchestration tool, designed to simplify the management of containerized workloads and provide built-in support for high availability, load balancing, and service discovery. To set up a Docker Swarm cluster, users first need to prepare their Docker hosts by installing Docker Engine and enabling the Swarm mode. This can be done by running the following command on each host:

bashCopy code

```
docker swarm init --advertise-addr <manager-ip>
```

This command initializes the Docker Swarm mode on the host and designates it as the Swarm manager, which is responsible for orchestrating container deployments and managing cluster resources. The **--advertise-addr** flag specifies the IP address of the host that other nodes in the cluster will use to communicate with the Swarm manager. Once the Swarm manager is initialized, users can join additional Docker hosts to the Swarm cluster as worker nodes using the following command:

bashCopy code

```
docker swarm join --token <swarm-token> <manager-ip>:<manager-port>
```

This command generates a join token that allows the host to join the Swarm cluster as a worker node and connects it to the specified Swarm manager using its IP address and port. With the Swarm cluster set up and all nodes joined, users can verify the status of the cluster and view information about the Swarm manager and worker nodes using the following command:

bashCopy code

```
docker node ls
```

This command lists all nodes in the Swarm cluster, including their IDs, hostnames, statuses, and availability, providing users with an overview of the cluster topology and status. Additionally, users can inspect individual nodes in the cluster and view detailed information about their configuration and resources using the following command:

bashCopy code

```
docker node inspect <node-id>
```

This command displays detailed information about the specified node, including its ID, hostname, IP address, status, and available resources such as CPU, memory, and storage. With the Docker Swarm cluster set up and all nodes joined, users can deploy containerized applications onto the cluster using Docker services. A Docker service is a scalable and resilient unit of deployment that defines how a containerized application should be run and managed within the Swarm cluster. Users can create a new Docker service and deploy it onto the Swarm cluster using the following command:

bashCopy code

```
docker service create --name <service-name> --replicas <num-replicas> <image-name>
```

This command creates a new Docker service with the specified name and number of replicas and deploys the specified container image onto the Swarm cluster. The replicas parameter specifies the desired number of instances of the service to run across the cluster, enabling users to scale the service horizontally and distribute its workload evenly across multiple nodes. Once the service is created, Docker Swarm automatically schedules the service tasks onto available worker nodes in the cluster and manages their lifecycle, ensuring high availability and fault tolerance. Users can monitor the status and health of Docker services using the following command:

bashCopy code

```
docker service ls
```

This command lists all services deployed onto the Swarm cluster, including their names, replicas, image names, and running tasks, providing users with real-time visibility into the status and performance of their containerized applications. Additionally, users can inspect individual services and view detailed information about their configuration, tasks, and endpoints using the following command:

bashCopy code

```
docker service inspect <service-name>
```

This command displays detailed information about the specified service, including its ID, name, mode, replicas, image name, and labels, as well as a list of tasks associated with the service and their status. In summary, setting up a Docker Swarm cluster is a straightforward process that involves initializing the Swarm mode on a Docker host, joining additional hosts to the cluster, and deploying containerized applications onto the cluster using Docker services. With its built-in support for high availability, scalability, and fault tolerance, Docker Swarm provides users with a powerful platform for orchestrating and managing containerized workloads across a distributed cluster of Docker hosts.

Service Scaling and Rolling Updates are essential features of Docker Swarm, enabling users to dynamically adjust the number of replicas for a service and seamlessly update containerized applications without downtime or service disruption. Docker Swarm provides built-in support for scaling services horizontally by adding or removing replicas, allowing users to dynamically adjust the capacity of their applications to meet changing demand. To scale a Docker service in Swarm mode, users can use the **docker service scale** command, specifying the desired number of replicas for the service. For example, to scale a service named **my-web-app** to five replicas, users can execute the following command:

bashCopy code

```
docker service scale my-web-app=5
```

This command instructs Docker Swarm to adjust the number of replicas for the **my-web-app** service to five, effectively increasing its capacity and distributing its workload across multiple containers. Docker Swarm automatically schedules the new replicas onto available worker nodes in the cluster, ensuring that the service remains highly available and responsive to incoming requests. Additionally, Docker Swarm provides support for rolling updates, allowing users to update containerized applications one replica at a time while maintaining service availability and uptime. Rolling updates involve gradually replacing old containers with new ones, ensuring that the application remains accessible and functional throughout the update process. To perform a rolling update for a Docker service in Swarm mode, users can use the **docker service update** command, specifying the desired image to use for the update. For example, to update a service named **my-web-app** to use a new version of the container image **my-web-image:2.0**, users can execute the following command:

bashCopy code

```
docker service update --image my-web-image:2.0 my-web-app
```

This command instructs Docker Swarm to update the **my-web-app** service to use the specified container image **my-web-image:2.0**, triggering a rolling update process. During the rolling update, Docker Swarm replaces each old replica of the service with a new one based on the updated image, ensuring that the application remains available and responsive to incoming requests. Docker Swarm orchestrates the update process automatically, ensuring that only a subset of replicas is updated at any given time, minimizing the risk of service disruption or downtime. Additionally, Docker Swarm provides support for various update strategies, allowing users to control the pace and behavior of the rolling update process. For example, users can specify the **--update-parallelism** flag to define the maximum number of replicas that can be updated simultaneously, or use the **--update-delay** flag to introduce a delay between updates to allow for monitoring and validation. By leveraging these update strategies, users can fine-tune the rolling update process to meet their specific requirements and ensure smooth and efficient updates for their containerized applications. In summary, service scaling and rolling updates are essential features of Docker Swarm that enable users to dynamically adjust the capacity of their containerized applications and perform updates seamlessly without downtime or service disruption. By leveraging these features, users can ensure that their applications remain highly available, responsive, and resilient to changes in demand or application updates, providing a seamless experience for end users and stakeholders.

Chapter 3: Kubernetes Essentials for Docker Users

Introduction to Kubernetes Objects is essential for understanding the fundamental building blocks of Kubernetes and how they are used to define and manage applications in a Kubernetes cluster. Kubernetes objects are persistent entities in the Kubernetes system that represent the desired state of the cluster, including the applications, workloads, and resources running within it. These objects are defined using YAML or JSON configuration files and are submitted to the Kubernetes API server for processing and execution. One of the most common Kubernetes objects is the Pod, which represents the smallest deployable unit in Kubernetes and encapsulates one or more containers that share the same network namespace and storage volumes. To create a Pod in Kubernetes, users can define a Pod manifest file containing the desired configuration and submit it to the Kubernetes API server using the **kubectl apply** command.

bashCopy code

```
kubectl apply -f pod.yaml
```

This command instructs the Kubernetes API server to create or update the Pod defined in the **pod.yaml** manifest file, ensuring that the desired state of the Pod is maintained within the cluster. Another essential Kubernetes object is the Service, which provides network access to a set of Pods and enables load balancing and service discovery within the cluster. To create a Service in Kubernetes, users can define a Service manifest file containing the desired configuration and submit it to the Kubernetes API server using the **kubectl apply** command.

bashCopy code

```
kubectl apply -f service.yaml
```

This command instructs the Kubernetes API server to create or update the Service defined in the **service.yaml** manifest file, ensuring that the desired network configuration and access policies are applied within the cluster. In addition to Pods and Services, Kubernetes supports various other objects for defining and managing applications and resources within the cluster. For example, the Deployment object is used to manage the lifecycle of application deployments in Kubernetes, providing features such as rolling updates, scaling, and automated rollout and rollback.

bashCopy code

```
kubectl apply -f deployment.yaml
```

This command instructs the Kubernetes API server to create or update the Deployment defined in the **deployment.yaml** manifest file, ensuring that the desired number of replica Pods are running and that any changes to the application configuration are applied smoothly and efficiently. Similarly, the ConfigMap and Secret objects are used to manage configuration data and sensitive information within the cluster, allowing users to decouple configuration from application logic and manage secrets securely.

bashCopy code

```
kubectl apply -f configmap.yaml kubectl apply -f secret.yaml
```

These commands instruct the Kubernetes API server to create or update the ConfigMap and Secret defined in the respective manifest files, ensuring that the desired configuration data and sensitive information are available to the Pods and applications within the cluster. Overall, Kubernetes objects play a critical role in defining and managing the state of applications and resources within a Kubernetes cluster, providing a declarative and scalable approach to application deployment and management. By leveraging Kubernetes objects, users can define complex application topologies and deployment workflows in a concise and portable manner, enabling seamless deployment and management of containerized applications across diverse Kubernetes environments.

Deploying Applications with Kubernetes is a fundamental aspect of managing containerized workloads in a Kubernetes cluster, providing users with a scalable and resilient platform for running distributed applications. Kubernetes offers various mechanisms and tools for deploying applications, including Pods, Deployments, Services, and Ingress resources, each serving a specific purpose in the application deployment process. At the core of Kubernetes deployment is the Pod, which represents the smallest deployable unit in Kubernetes and encapsulates one or more containers that share the same network namespace and storage volumes. To deploy an application as a Pod in

Kubernetes, users can define a Pod manifest file containing the desired configuration and submit it to the Kubernetes API server using the **kubectl apply** command.

bashCopy code

```
kubectl apply -f pod.yaml
```

This command instructs the Kubernetes API server to create or update the Pod defined in the **pod.yaml** manifest file, ensuring that the desired state of the Pod is maintained within the cluster. However, directly managing Pods is not always the preferred approach for deploying applications in Kubernetes, as it lacks certain features such as scalability, rolling updates, and self-healing capabilities. Instead, users often use higher-level Kubernetes objects such as Deployments to manage the lifecycle of their applications more effectively. A Deployment in Kubernetes is a higher-level abstraction that manages a set of replica Pods and provides features such as rolling updates, scaling, and automated rollout and rollback. To deploy an application as a Deployment in Kubernetes, users can define a Deployment manifest file containing the desired configuration and submit it to the Kubernetes API server using the **kubectl apply** command.

bashCopy code

```
kubectl apply -f deployment.yaml
```

This command instructs the Kubernetes API server to create or update the Deployment defined in the **deployment.yaml** manifest file, ensuring that the desired number of replica Pods are running and that any changes to the application configuration are applied smoothly and efficiently. Deployments are ideal for managing stateless applications that can be scaled horizontally by adding or removing replica Pods, ensuring high availability and performance. However, for applications that require stateful behavior or data persistence, users can leverage other Kubernetes objects such as StatefulSets or DaemonSets. StatefulSets are used to manage stateful applications with unique identities and persistent storage requirements, ensuring that Pods are created and scaled in a predictable and consistent manner.

bashCopy code

```
kubectl apply -f statefulset.yaml
```

This command instructs the Kubernetes API server to create or update the StatefulSet defined in the **statefulset.yaml** manifest file, ensuring that the desired number of replica Pods are running and that any changes to the application configuration are applied smoothly and efficiently. StatefulSets are commonly used for databases, caches, and other stateful applications that require stable network identities and persistent storage. On the other hand, DaemonSets are used to manage daemons or system services that need to run on every node in the Kubernetes cluster, such as log collectors, monitoring agents, or networking proxies. To deploy an application as a DaemonSet in Kubernetes, users can define a DaemonSet manifest file containing the desired configuration and submit it to the Kubernetes API server using the **kubectl apply** command.

bashCopy code

```bash
kubectl apply -f daemonset.yaml
```

This command instructs the Kubernetes API server to create or update the DaemonSet defined in the **daemonset.yaml** manifest file, ensuring that the specified Pods are scheduled and running on every node in the cluster. DaemonSets are useful for deploying system-level services or utilities that need to run alongside user applications on every node in the cluster, ensuring consistent behavior and resource utilization across the entire cluster. In addition to managing application workloads, Kubernetes also provides mechanisms for exposing applications to external users or clients through Services and Ingress resources. A Service in Kubernetes is an abstraction that defines a logical set of Pods and a policy for accessing them, providing features such as load balancing, service discovery, and internal network routing.

bashCopy code

```bash
kubectl apply -f service.yaml
```

This command instructs the Kubernetes API server to create or update the Service defined in the **service.yaml** manifest file, ensuring that the specified Pods are accessible to clients within the cluster. Services can be of different types, such as ClusterIP, NodePort, or LoadBalancer, each serving a specific purpose in the application deployment process. For example, a ClusterIP Service exposes Pods internally within the cluster, while a NodePort Service exposes Pods externally by mapping a port on every node in the cluster. Lastly, an Ingress resource in Kubernetes is used to expose HTTP and HTTPS routes from outside the cluster to Services within the cluster, providing features such as path-based routing, TLS termination, and virtual hosting.

bashCopy code

```
kubectl apply -f ingress.yaml
```

This command instructs the Kubernetes API server to create or update the Ingress resource defined in the **ingress.yaml** manifest file, ensuring that the specified HTTP or HTTPS routes are mapped to the appropriate Services within the cluster. Ingress resources are commonly used for exposing web applications or APIs to external users or clients, providing a flexible and scalable approach to external access and traffic management. In summary, deploying applications with Kubernetes involves defining and managing various Kubernetes objects such as Pods, Deployments, Services, and Ingress resources, each serving a specific purpose in the application deployment process. By leveraging these Kubernetes objects and tools, users can deploy and manage containerized applications in a scalable, resilient, and efficient manner, ensuring high availability, performance, and security across diverse Kubernetes environments.

Chapter 4: Docker Security Best Practices

Securing Docker Daemon and Containers is crucial for maintaining the integrity and confidentiality of applications and data running within Docker environments. Docker provides several built-in security features and best practices that users can leverage to mitigate risks and protect against potential threats. One of the first steps in securing Docker environments is to ensure that the Docker daemon is configured with appropriate security settings and permissions. Docker daemon configuration is typically managed through the Docker daemon configuration file, which is located at **/etc/docker/daemon.json** on Linux systems. Users can edit this file to specify various security-related settings, such as restricting network access, limiting resource usage, and enabling Docker Content Trust. To edit the Docker daemon configuration file, users can use a text editor such as **nano** or **vi** to open the file and make the necessary changes.

bashCopy code

```
nano /etc/docker/daemon.json
```

This command opens the Docker daemon configuration file in the **nano** text editor, allowing users to modify the configuration settings as needed. Once the configuration changes have been made, users can save the file and exit the text editor to apply the changes to the Docker daemon. Additionally, Docker provides built-in support for Docker Content Trust (DCT), a feature that enables image signing and verification to ensure the authenticity and integrity of container images. DCT uses cryptographic signatures to verify the publisher and integrity of container images before they are pulled and executed on Docker hosts. To enable Docker Content Trust, users can set the **DOCKER_CONTENT_TRUST** environment variable to **1** to enable image signing and verification globally.

bashCopy code

```
export DOCKER_CONTENT_TRUST=1
```

This command sets the **DOCKER_CONTENT_TRUST** environment variable to **1**, enabling Docker Content Trust globally for all Docker operations performed on the host. With Docker Content Trust enabled, Docker will automatically verify the authenticity and integrity of container images before pulling and executing them on Docker hosts, helping to prevent the execution of tampered or malicious images. Another critical aspect of securing Docker environments is to implement container runtime security measures to protect against runtime threats and attacks. Docker provides several security features and best practices that users can leverage to enhance container runtime security, such as using Docker Security Scanning, enabling AppArmor or SELinux, and implementing least privilege principles.

bashCopy code

```
docker scan <image-name>
```

This command uses Docker Security Scanning to analyze the specified container image for known vulnerabilities and security issues, providing users with actionable insights and recommendations for improving container security. Docker Security Scanning integrates with Docker Hub and other container registries to provide real-time vulnerability scanning and security analysis for container images, helping users identify and remediate security risks before deploying them in production environments. Additionally, users can leverage Linux security modules such as AppArmor or SELinux to implement mandatory access control policies and enforce fine-grained access controls on container processes and resources.

bashCopy code

```
docker run --security-opt apparmor=profile <image-name>
```

This command launches a container using the specified AppArmor profile, enforcing the security policy defined in the profile and restricting the container's access to system resources and sensitive files. Similarly, users can use SELinux to enforce mandatory access controls and security policies on container processes and resources, helping to prevent unauthorized access and mitigate the impact of potential security breaches. Furthermore, implementing the principle of least privilege is essential for reducing the attack surface and minimizing the potential impact of security vulnerabilities and exploits. Users should follow best practices for container image security, such as using minimal and hardened base images, removing unnecessary dependencies and packages, and running containers with minimal privileges and permissions.

bashCopy code

```
docker run --cap-drop=all --security-opt no-new-privileges <image-name>
```

This command launches a container with minimal privileges and permissions, dropping all Linux capabilities and enforcing the **no-new-privileges** security option to prevent privilege escalation and container breakout attacks. By following these security best practices and implementing appropriate security measures, users can enhance the security posture of Docker environments and protect against a wide range of security threats and attacks. Additionally, regular security audits, vulnerability assessments, and penetration testing are essential for identifying and addressing security weaknesses and vulnerabilities in Docker deployments, ensuring that containerized applications and data remain secure and compliant with industry standards and regulations. In summary, securing Docker daemon and containers involves implementing various security measures and best practices, such as configuring Docker daemon with appropriate security settings, enabling Docker Content Trust, implementing container runtime security measures, and following security best practices for container image management and deployment. By adopting a holistic approach to container security and incorporating security into every stage of the container lifecycle, users can enhance the security posture of Docker environments and protect against potential threats and attacks.

Implementing Role-Based Access Control (RBAC) is essential for managing access to resources and securing Kubernetes clusters effectively. RBAC allows administrators to define granular access policies and permissions based on user roles, enabling fine-grained control over who can perform specific actions within the cluster. Kubernetes provides built-in support for RBAC, allowing users to define custom roles, role bindings, and cluster roles to enforce access control policies at the namespace or cluster level. One of the first steps in implementing RBAC in Kubernetes is to define custom roles that specify the permissions and actions that users or groups are allowed to perform within a namespace. Users can define custom roles using YAML manifest files that specify the API resources, verbs, and resource names that the role grants access to.

bashCopy code

```
kubectl create -f custom-role.yaml
```

This command creates a custom role in the Kubernetes cluster based on the specifications defined in the **custom-role.yaml** manifest file, granting the specified permissions to users or groups within the specified namespace. Once the custom roles have been defined, users can create role bindings to associate the roles with specific users, groups, or service accounts within the cluster. Role bindings link a role to one or more subjects, such as users or groups, granting them the permissions specified by the role.

bashCopy code

```
kubectl create rolebinding <role-binding-name> --role=<role-name> --user=<username>
```

This command creates a role binding in the Kubernetes cluster, associating the specified role with the specified user, and granting them the permissions defined by the role. Additionally, Kubernetes provides built-in roles and cluster roles that users can leverage to grant common sets of permissions to users or groups within the cluster. Built-in roles are predefined sets of permissions that grant access to specific resources and API operations within a namespace, while cluster roles provide access to cluster-wide resources and operations across all namespaces.

bashCopy code

```
kubectl create clusterrolebinding <cluster-role-binding-name> --clusterrole=<cluster-role-name> --user=<username>
```

This command creates a cluster role binding in the Kubernetes cluster, associating the specified cluster role with the specified user, and granting them the permissions defined by the cluster role. Cluster roles are typically used to grant broader permissions that apply across all namespaces in the cluster, such as cluster administration or management tasks. In addition to defining custom roles and role bindings, users can also leverage Kubernetes' attribute-based access control (ABAC) mechanism to enforce access control policies based on user attributes or labels.

bashCopy code

```
kubectl create -f abac-policy.yaml --dry-run=client -o yaml | sed "s/namespace: default/namespace: <namespace>/g" | kubectl apply -f -
```

This command applies an ABAC policy to the specified namespace in the Kubernetes cluster, enforcing access control policies based on user attributes or labels defined in the policy. ABAC allows administrators to define access control rules based on user attributes such as usernames, group memberships, or labels assigned to users or objects within the cluster. By leveraging RBAC and ABAC together, users can implement robust access control policies that enforce the principle of least privilege and ensure that only authorized users have access to sensitive resources and operations within the Kubernetes cluster. Additionally, Kubernetes provides audit logging and monitoring capabilities that allow administrators to track and monitor user activity and access patterns within the cluster.

bashCopy code

```
kubectl logs <audit-log-pod-name> -n <audit-log-namespace>
```

This command retrieves the audit logs from the specified pod in the specified namespace, allowing administrators to monitor and analyze user activity and access patterns within the Kubernetes cluster. By enabling audit logging and monitoring, administrators can gain visibility into user actions and access requests, detect unauthorized or suspicious activity, and enforce compliance with security policies and regulations. In summary, implementing Role-Based Access Control (RBAC) in Kubernetes is essential for managing access to resources and securing Kubernetes clusters effectively. By defining custom roles, role bindings, and cluster roles, users can enforce granular access control policies that restrict access to sensitive resources and operations based on user roles and permissions. Additionally, leveraging attribute-based access control (ABAC) and audit logging capabilities allows administrators to monitor and track user activity within the cluster, ensuring compliance with security policies and regulations. By following best practices for RBAC implementation and access control management, users can enhance the security posture of Kubernetes clusters and protect against unauthorized access and data breaches.

Chapter 5: Dockerizing Microservices Architectures

Designing Microservices for Docker Containers requires careful consideration of various architectural principles and best practices to ensure scalability, resilience, and maintainability in distributed systems. Microservices architecture decomposes applications into small, independent services that can be developed, deployed, and scaled independently, making it an ideal fit for containerized environments like Docker. One of the key principles of designing microservices for Docker containers is service decomposition, where applications are broken down into smaller, loosely coupled services that can be developed and deployed independently.

bashCopy code

```
docker-compose up -d
```

This command launches the Docker containers defined in the **docker-compose.yml** file, enabling developers to test and validate the functionality of individual microservices in isolation. By decomposing applications into smaller services, developers can improve agility, scalability, and maintainability, as each service can be developed, tested, and deployed independently without impacting other services. Additionally, designing microservices with a focus on bounded contexts helps define clear boundaries and responsibilities for each service, ensuring that each service is responsible for a specific set of business capabilities or functions.

bashCopy code

```
docker swarm init
```

This command initializes a Docker Swarm cluster, enabling developers to deploy and manage microservices across multiple Docker hosts in a distributed and scalable manner. Docker Swarm provides built-in support for service discovery, load balancing, and rolling updates, making it an ideal platform for deploying microservices in production environments. Another key consideration when designing microservices for Docker containers is resilience and fault tolerance, where each service should be designed to handle failures gracefully and recover quickly in the event of an outage or disruption.

bashCopy code

```
docker service scale <service-name>=<replica-count>
```

This command scales the specified service in the Docker Swarm cluster to the specified number of replicas, enabling developers to adjust the capacity of microservices dynamically based on workload demand. By designing microservices with resilience and fault tolerance in mind, developers can improve the overall reliability and availability of distributed systems, ensuring that services remain responsive and accessible even in the face of failures or disruptions. Additionally, designing microservices with a focus on loose coupling and asynchronous communication helps minimize dependencies between services, allowing them to evolve independently over time without causing disruptions or bottlenecks.

bashCopy code

```
docker-compose logs <service-name>
```

This command retrieves the logs for the specified microservice from the Docker containers, enabling developers to monitor and troubleshoot issues in real-time. By designing microservices with loose coupling and asynchronous communication, developers can improve scalability, flexibility, and agility, as each service can evolve independently without requiring coordination or synchronization with other services. Furthermore, designing microservices with a focus on statelessness and idempotency helps improve scalability and fault tolerance, as stateless services can be easily replicated and scaled horizontally to handle increasing workloads.

bashCopy code

```
docker stack deploy -c <stack-file> <stack-name>
```

This command deploys the Docker stack defined in the specified stack file to the Docker Swarm cluster, enabling developers to deploy and manage multiple microservices as a single unit. By encapsulating related microservices within a Docker stack, developers can simplify deployment and management tasks, as well as ensure consistency and version compatibility across services. Additionally, designing microservices with observability in mind helps improve visibility and troubleshooting capabilities, as developers can monitor and track the performance and behavior of microservices in real-time.

bashCopy code

```
docker stats <container-id>
```

This command retrieves the resource usage statistics for the specified Docker container, enabling developers to monitor and optimize the performance of microservices in production environments. By designing microservices with observability in mind, developers can gain insights into the health, performance, and behavior of microservices, enabling them to identify and address performance bottlenecks, resource constraints, and reliability issues proactively. In summary, designing microservices for Docker containers requires a holistic approach that considers various architectural principles and best practices, including service decomposition, bounded contexts, resilience, fault tolerance, loose coupling, asynchronous communication, statelessness, idempotency, encapsulation, observability, and scalability. By following these principles and leveraging Docker's capabilities, developers can design and deploy microservices that are resilient, scalable, and maintainable in containerized environments.

Containerizing legacy applications is a critical step in modernizing traditional monolithic systems and unlocking the benefits of containerization, such as portability, scalability, and agility. Legacy applications, often built using outdated technologies and architectures, can present challenges when migrating to containerized environments like Docker. However, with the right approach and tools, legacy applications can be containerized successfully, enabling organizations to leverage modern cloud-native technologies and practices while preserving existing investments in legacy systems. One of the first steps in containerizing legacy applications is to assess the application's architecture and dependencies to identify potential challenges and compatibility issues.

bashCopy code

```
docker run --name <container-name> -v /path/to/application:/app <image-name>
```

This command runs the legacy application in a Docker container, mounting the application files and dependencies from the host system into the container's filesystem. By running the legacy application in a Docker container, developers can test its compatibility and behavior in a containerized environment, identifying any dependencies or configuration issues that need to be addressed before migrating to production. Additionally, developers can leverage Docker's build capabilities to create Docker images for legacy applications, encapsulating the application code, dependencies, and configuration in a portable and reproducible format.

bashCopy code

```
docker build -t <image-name> .
```

This command builds a Docker image for the legacy application using the Dockerfile and application files located in the current directory. By creating Docker images for legacy applications, developers can package and distribute the applications as self-contained units that can be deployed and run consistently across different environments, such as development, testing, and production. Furthermore, containerizing legacy applications enables organizations to take advantage of Docker's orchestration capabilities, such as Docker Swarm or Kubernetes, to deploy and manage the applications at scale in distributed environments.

bashCopy code

```
docker-compose up -d
```

This command deploys the legacy application as a Docker service using Docker Compose, enabling developers to define and manage multi-container applications with a single configuration file. By using Docker Compose, developers can specify the dependencies and configuration for the legacy application, such as environment variables, network settings, and volume mounts, in a declarative manner, simplifying the deployment and management of complex applications. Additionally, Docker Compose provides built-in support for service discovery, load balancing, and rolling updates, making it an ideal tool for deploying legacy applications in production environments.

bashCopy code

```bash
docker swarm init
```

This command initializes a Docker Swarm cluster, enabling developers to deploy and manage legacy applications across multiple Docker hosts in a distributed and scalable manner. Docker Swarm provides built-in support for high availability, fault tolerance, and auto-scaling, allowing organizations to run legacy applications reliably and efficiently in production environments. Moreover, containerizing legacy applications enables organizations to adopt modern DevOps practices and CI/CD pipelines, streamlining the application development and deployment lifecycle.

bashCopy code

```bash
docker push <image-name>
```

This command pushes the Docker image for the legacy application to a container registry, such as Docker Hub or Amazon ECR, enabling developers to share and distribute the image with other team members or deploy it to production environments. By using container registries, organizations can version control and manage Docker images centrally, ensuring consistency and traceability across different environments. Additionally, containerizing legacy applications facilitates the adoption of cloud-native architectures and microservices, enabling organizations to decompose monolithic applications into smaller, more manageable services that can be developed, deployed, and scaled independently.

bashCopy code

```bash
docker service scale <service-name>=<replica-count>
```

This command scales the legacy application service in the Docker Swarm cluster to the specified number of replicas, enabling organizations to adjust the capacity of the application dynamically based on workload demand. By scaling legacy applications horizontally with Docker Swarm, organizations can improve performance, reliability, and resource utilization, ensuring that the applications can handle increasing traffic and workload spikes efficiently. In summary, containerizing legacy applications is a transformative process that enables organizations to modernize their IT infrastructure and unlock the benefits of containerization and cloud-native technologies. By leveraging Docker and related tools, organizations can migrate legacy applications to containerized environments seamlessly, enabling greater agility, scalability, and resilience in today's fast-paced digital world.

Chapter 6: Continuous Integration and Deployment with Docker

Integrating Docker with Continuous Integration/Continuous Deployment (CI/CD) pipelines is essential for streamlining the software development lifecycle and enabling automated testing, deployment, and delivery of containerized applications. CI/CD pipelines automate the process of building, testing, and deploying software changes, enabling organizations to deliver high-quality software quickly and reliably. Docker plays a crucial role in CI/CD pipelines by providing a standardized and portable runtime environment for applications, ensuring consistency and reproducibility across different stages of the pipeline. One of the key steps in integrating Docker with CI/CD pipelines is to define Dockerfiles for each application component, specifying the dependencies, environment variables, and commands required to build the Docker images.

bashCopy code

```
docker build -t <image-name> .
```

This command builds a Docker image for the application using the Dockerfile located in the current directory, enabling developers to package the application and its dependencies into a portable and reproducible format. By defining Dockerfiles, developers can automate the process of building

Docker images as part of the CI/CD pipeline, ensuring that applications are built consistently and efficiently across different environments. Additionally, Docker images can be tagged with version numbers or Git commit hashes to track changes and enable rollback to previous versions if needed.

bashCopy code

```
docker push <image-name>
```

This command pushes the Docker image for the application to a container registry, such as Docker Hub or Amazon ECR, enabling developers to share and distribute the image with other team members or deploy it to production environments. By using container registries, organizations can version control and manage Docker images centrally, ensuring consistency and traceability across different environments. Moreover, integrating Docker with CI/CD pipelines enables organizations to automate the testing of Docker images using containerized testing frameworks and tools, such as Docker Compose or Kubernetes.

bashCopy code

```
docker-compose -f docker-compose.test.yml up --abort-on-container-exit
```

This command spins up the test environment defined in the **docker-compose.test.yml** file, enabling developers to run automated tests against the Dockerized application components. By using Docker Compose, developers can define multi-container test environments that closely resemble production environments, allowing them to validate the functionality and performance of the application in a controlled and reproducible manner. Additionally, Docker Compose provides built-in support for service dependencies, environment variables, and volume mounts, making it easy to configure and manage complex test environments.

bashCopy code

```
docker run --rm <image-name> npm test
```

This command runs the test suite for the Dockerized application component in a temporary Docker container, enabling developers to execute unit tests or integration tests against the application code. By running tests in isolated Docker containers, developers can ensure that tests are executed in a clean and reproducible environment, minimizing the risk of environment-specific issues or dependencies. Furthermore, integrating Docker with CI/CD pipelines enables organizations to automate the deployment of Docker images to staging and production environments using container orchestration platforms like Kubernetes or Docker Swarm.

bashCopy code

```
kubectl apply -f deployment.yaml
```

This command deploys the Docker image for the application to a Kubernetes cluster using the deployment manifest defined in the **deployment.yaml** file, enabling organizations to automate the deployment process and ensure consistency across different environments. By using Kubernetes' declarative deployment model, organizations can define the desired state of the application and let Kubernetes handle the details of deploying and managing the application replicas, scaling, and rolling updates. Additionally, Kubernetes provides built-in support for health checks, self-healing, and service discovery, making it an ideal platform for running containerized applications in production environments.

bashCopy code

```
docker service update --image <image-name>:<tag>
<service-name>
```

This command updates the Docker service running in a Docker Swarm cluster with the new Docker image specified by the image name and tag, enabling organizations to automate the deployment of new application versions and perform rolling updates without downtime. By using Docker Swarm's built-in rolling update capabilities, organizations can update application replicas one by one, ensuring high availability and reliability of the application during the deployment process. Moreover, integrating Docker with CI/CD pipelines enables organizations to monitor and track the performance and health of Dockerized applications using container monitoring and logging tools.

bashCopy code

```
docker stats <container-id>
```

This command retrieves the resource usage statistics for the specified Docker container, enabling organizations to monitor and optimize the performance of Dockerized applications in production environments. By using container monitoring tools, organizations can gain insights into the CPU, memory, and network usage of Docker containers, identify performance bottlenecks, and troubleshoot issues proactively. In summary, integrating Docker with CI/CD pipelines enables organizations to automate the build, test, and deployment processes of containerized applications, ensuring consistency, reliability, and scalability across different stages of the software development lifecycle. By leveraging Docker's capabilities and ecosystem of tools, organizations can streamline the delivery of high-quality software and accelerate their time-to-market in today's fast-paced digital world.

Automated deployment strategies are essential for modern software development practices, enabling organizations to streamline the process of releasing software changes to production environments efficiently and reliably. Automated deployment strategies encompass a range of techniques and tools that automate the deployment process, reducing manual effort, minimizing human error, and accelerating the time-to-market for software releases. One of the key automated deployment strategies is Continuous Deployment (CD), which involves automatically deploying every code change to production environments after passing automated tests. Continuous Deployment relies on automated testing frameworks and CI/CD pipelines to validate code changes and ensure that only quality-tested changes are deployed to production.

bashCopy code

```
git push origin <branch-name>
```

This command pushes code changes to the remote Git repository, triggering the CI/CD pipeline to build, test, and deploy the changes automatically. By using version control systems like Git and CI/CD pipelines, organizations can automate the process of deploying code changes to production environments, ensuring consistency and reliability across different stages of the deployment pipeline. Moreover, automated deployment strategies enable organizations to implement canary releases, where new code changes are gradually rolled out to a small percentage of users before being fully deployed to production.

bashCopy code

```
kubectl set image deployment/<deployment-name> <container-name>=<new-image>:<tag>
```

This command updates the Docker image for the specified container in a Kubernetes deployment, enabling organizations to perform rolling updates and automate the deployment of new application versions. By using Kubernetes' declarative deployment model and rolling update capabilities, organizations can update application replicas one by one, ensuring high availability and reliability of the application during the deployment process. Additionally, automated deployment strategies enable organizations to implement feature toggles, allowing developers to enable or disable new features dynamically without deploying code changes.

bashCopy code

```
docker stack deploy -c <stack-file> <stack-name>
```

This command deploys a Docker stack defined in the specified Compose file to a Docker Swarm cluster, enabling organizations to automate the deployment of multi-container applications. By using Docker Swarm's built-in support for rolling updates and service discovery, organizations can deploy and manage complex applications at scale, ensuring consistency and reliability across different environments. Moreover, automated deployment strategies enable organizations to implement blue-green deployments, where new application versions are deployed alongside existing versions and traffic is gradually switched to the new version.

bashCopy code

```
helm upgrade --install <release-name> <chart-name>
--namespace <namespace> --set <values>
```

This command upgrades or installs a Helm chart in a Kubernetes cluster, enabling organizations to automate the deployment of applications and manage their dependencies easily. By using Helm, organizations can define application configurations and dependencies in a single chart file, simplifying the deployment and management of complex applications. Additionally, automated deployment strategies enable organizations to implement Infrastructure as Code (IaC) principles, where infrastructure configurations are defined and managed using code, enabling organizations to automate the provisioning and configuration of infrastructure resources.

bashCopy code

```
aws cloudformation deploy --template-file <template-file> --stack-name <stack-name> --capabilities CAPABILITY_IAM
```

This command deploys an AWS CloudFormation stack using the specified template file, enabling organizations to automate the provisioning and configuration of AWS resources. By using CloudFormation, organizations can define infrastructure resources and their dependencies in a template file, enabling them to provision and manage infrastructure resources consistently and reliably. Moreover, automated deployment strategies enable organizations to implement automated rollback mechanisms, where deployments are automatically rolled back to previous versions in case of failures or issues.

bashCopy code

```
ansible-playbook <playbook-file> -i <inventory-file>
```

This command runs an Ansible playbook to automate the deployment and configuration of infrastructure resources and applications, enabling organizations to implement Infrastructure as Code (IaC) principles. By using Ansible, organizations can define infrastructure configurations and application deployments in a playbook file, enabling them to automate repetitive tasks and ensure consistency across different environments. Additionally, automated deployment strategies enable organizations to implement automated testing and validation processes, where deployments are automatically tested against predefined criteria before being promoted to production.

bashCopy code

```
terraform apply
```

This command applies the changes defined in a Terraform configuration file to provision or update infrastructure resources in a cloud environment, enabling organizations to automate the deployment and management of infrastructure resources. By using Terraform, organizations can define infrastructure configurations in a declarative manner and manage infrastructure resources as code, enabling them to automate the provisioning and configuration of infrastructure resources across different cloud providers. Furthermore, automated deployment strategies enable organizations to implement deployment pipelines as code, where deployment processes are defined and managed using version-controlled configuration files.

bashCopy code

```
jenkins-cli create-job <job-name> <config-file>
```

This command creates a Jenkins job using the specified configuration file, enabling organizations to automate the deployment and management of CI/CD pipelines. By using Jenkins, organizations can define and orchestrate complex deployment pipelines that automate the process of building, testing, and deploying software changes to production environments. Additionally, automated deployment strategies enable organizations to implement automated monitoring and alerting processes, where deployments are automatically monitored for performance and availability metrics, and alerts are triggered in case of issues or anomalies. In summary, automated deployment strategies enable organizations to streamline the software delivery process, accelerate the time-to-market for software releases, and improve the reliability and scalability of production environments. By leveraging automation tools and techniques, organizations can achieve greater agility, efficiency, and competitiveness in today's fast-paced digital world.

Chapter 7: Monitoring and Logging in Docker Environments

Container metrics and monitoring tools play a crucial role in managing and maintaining the health, performance, and availability of containerized applications in production environments. As organizations increasingly adopt container orchestration platforms like Kubernetes and Docker Swarm, the need for robust monitoring solutions to track container metrics and diagnose performance issues becomes paramount. Container metrics provide valuable insights into the resource utilization, performance, and behavior of containers, enabling organizations to optimize resource allocation, troubleshoot issues, and ensure the reliability of containerized applications. One of the fundamental metrics to monitor in containerized environments is resource utilization, including CPU, memory, and disk usage, which can be measured using built-in container monitoring tools or third-party monitoring solutions.

bashCopy code

```
docker stats <container-id>
```

This command retrieves real-time resource usage statistics for the specified Docker container, including CPU, memory, and network metrics, enabling operators to monitor the health and performance of containers in production environments. By using built-in Docker commands like **docker stats**, operators can gain insights into the resource utilization patterns of containers, identify performance bottlenecks, and optimize resource allocation to improve application performance and scalability. Additionally, container metrics provide visibility into the lifecycle of containers, including start time, uptime, and restart count, allowing operators to track container health and availability over time.

bashCopy code

```
kubectl top pods --namespace <namespace>
```

This command retrieves resource usage statistics for Kubernetes pods in the specified namespace, including CPU and memory usage, enabling operators to monitor the resource consumption of applications running in Kubernetes clusters. By using the **kubectl top** command, operators can identify pods that are consuming excessive resources or experiencing performance issues, allowing them to take corrective actions, such as scaling or restarting pods, to ensure the stability and availability of applications. Moreover, container metrics provide insights into container networking, including network bandwidth, latency, and errors, enabling operators to monitor network performance and troubleshoot connectivity issues.

bashCopy code

```
docker inspect <container-id>
```

This command retrieves detailed information about the specified Docker container, including configuration settings, network settings, and volume mounts, enabling operators to troubleshoot issues and debug containerized applications. By using the **docker inspect** command, operators can inspect the runtime environment of containers, including environment variables, command-line arguments, and process IDs, allowing them to identify misconfigurations or conflicts that may impact application performance or stability. Additionally, container metrics provide insights into container storage, including disk usage, storage volumes, and filesystem type, enabling operators to monitor storage consumption and optimize storage allocation for containers.

bashCopy code

```
prometheus-server --config <config-file>
```

This command starts the Prometheus server with the specified configuration file, enabling organizations to collect, store, and query container metrics from Prometheus exporters running in containerized environments. By using Prometheus, organizations can create custom dashboards and alerts to monitor container metrics, including resource utilization, application performance, and system health, enabling operators to detect and respond to issues proactively. Moreover, container metrics provide insights into application performance, including response time, throughput, and error rates, enabling organizations to monitor application health and troubleshoot performance issues in real-time.

bashCopy code

```
grafana-server --config <config-file>
```

This command starts the Grafana server with the specified configuration file, enabling organizations to visualize and analyze container metrics collected from Prometheus or other monitoring systems. By using Grafana, organizations can create custom dashboards and visualizations to monitor containerized applications, track key performance indicators (KPIs), and identify trends and anomalies in container metrics. Additionally, container metrics provide insights into container orchestration, including Kubernetes events, pod status, and node health, enabling operators to monitor the overall health and performance of Kubernetes clusters and troubleshoot issues efficiently.

bashCopy code

```
aws cloudwatch put-metric-data --namespace <namespace> --metric-name <metric-name> --value <value> --dimensions <dimensions>
```

This command publishes custom metrics to Amazon CloudWatch, enabling organizations to monitor containerized applications running in AWS environments. By using CloudWatch, organizations can collect and visualize container metrics, including CPU, memory, and disk usage, and set up alarms to alert operators about performance issues or failures. Moreover, container metrics provide insights into container orchestration, including Kubernetes events, pod status, and node health, enabling organizations to monitor the overall health and performance of Kubernetes clusters and troubleshoot issues efficiently.

bashCopy code

```
fluentd -c <config-file>
```

This command starts the Fluentd daemon with the specified configuration file, enabling organizations to collect, parse, and forward container logs to centralized logging systems like Elasticsearch or Splunk. By using Fluentd, organizations can aggregate and analyze container logs in real-time, enabling operators to troubleshoot issues, monitor application performance, and comply with regulatory requirements. Additionally, container metrics provide insights into container security, including vulnerabilities, runtime threats, and compliance violations, enabling organizations to detect and respond to security incidents in containerized environments.

bashCopy code

```
sysdig capture -o <output-file> container.name=<container-name>
```

This command starts a Sysdig capture session to monitor system calls and network activity for the specified Docker container, enabling operators to investigate security incidents or performance issues in containerized environments. By using Sysdig, organizations can capture detailed telemetry data from containers, including process activity, file access, and network connections, enabling operators to analyze and correlate events to identify anomalies or malicious activities. In summary, container metrics and monitoring tools are essential for managing and maintaining the health, performance, and security of containerized applications in production environments. By leveraging container metrics and monitoring solutions, organizations can gain visibility into containerized workloads, detect and respond to issues proactively, and ensure the reliability and scalability of containerized applications in today's dynamic and fast-paced IT environments.

Centralized logging solutions are indispensable components of modern IT infrastructures, providing organizations with the capability to aggregate, store, and analyze log data from various sources across their environments. As organizations increasingly adopt distributed architectures and microservices-based applications, the need for centralized logging solutions becomes even more critical to effectively monitor, troubleshoot, and secure their systems. Centralized logging solutions offer several benefits, including improved visibility, simplified troubleshooting, enhanced security, and compliance adherence. One of the key advantages of centralized logging solutions is their ability to aggregate log data from multiple sources, such as servers, containers, applications, and network devices, into a single, centralized repository.

bashCopy code

```bash
rsyslogd -f <config-file>
```

This command starts the Rsyslog daemon with the specified configuration file, enabling organizations to collect and forward log messages from Linux-based systems to a centralized logging server. By using Rsyslog, organizations can configure log forwarding rules and filters to route log messages to specific destinations, such as remote syslog servers or log management platforms. Additionally, Rsyslog supports various log formats and protocols, including syslog, JSON, and TLS, enabling organizations to customize their logging configurations based on their requirements and preferences.

bashCopy code

```bash
fluentd -c <config-file>
```

This command starts the Fluentd daemon with the specified configuration file, enabling organizations to collect, parse, and forward log data from various sources, including applications, containers, and cloud platforms, to centralized logging systems like Elasticsearch, Splunk, or Kafka. By using Fluentd, organizations can standardize log formats, enrich log data with additional metadata, and route log messages to multiple destinations simultaneously, enabling comprehensive log aggregation and analysis. Additionally, Fluentd supports a wide range of input and output plugins, allowing organizations to integrate with different log sources and destinations seamlessly.

bashCopy code

```
filebeat -e -c <config-file>
```

This command starts the Filebeat agent with the specified configuration file in 'elastic' output mode, enabling organizations to ship log data from files, containers, and other sources to Elasticsearch or Logstash for centralized storage and analysis. By using Filebeat, organizations can monitor log files in real-time, extract relevant log events, and forward them to the Elasticsearch cluster for indexing and search. Additionally, Filebeat supports various data transformation and enrichment capabilities, enabling organizations to parse, filter, and enhance log data before indexing it in Elasticsearch.

bashCopy code

```
logstash -f <config-file>
```

This command starts the Logstash service with the specified configuration file, enabling organizations to ingest, transform, and enrich log data from multiple sources before storing it in centralized logging systems like Elasticsearch or Splunk. By using Logstash, organizations can define custom data processing pipelines to parse, filter, and enrich log events, enabling advanced log aggregation and analysis. Additionally, Logstash supports a wide range of input and output plugins, including file inputs, TCP/UDP inputs, and Elasticsearch outputs, enabling flexible integration with different log sources and destinations.

bashCopy code

```
kinesis-agent -c <config-file>
```

This command starts the Kinesis Agent with the specified configuration file, enabling organizations to stream log data from EC2 instances, containers, and other AWS services to Amazon Kinesis Data Streams or Amazon CloudWatch Logs for centralized storage and analysis. By using the Kinesis Agent, organizations can configure log rotation, buffering, and error handling settings to ensure reliable and efficient log data ingestion into Amazon Kinesis or CloudWatch. Additionally, the Kinesis Agent supports multi-line log parsing and custom log formatting options, enabling organizations to handle complex log formats and structures.

bashCopy code

```
splunk add monitor <log-file>
```

This command configures Splunk to monitor the specified log file for changes and ingest new log events into the Splunk index for centralized storage and analysis. By using Splunk's monitoring capabilities, organizations can track log file changes in real-time, extract relevant log events, and index them in Splunk for search and analysis. Additionally, Splunk supports advanced search and visualization features, enabling organizations to gain insights into their log data, detect anomalies, and troubleshoot issues efficiently.

bashCopy code

```
syslog-ng -f <config-file>
```

This command starts the Syslog-ng service with the specified configuration file, enabling organizations to collect, filter, and forward log messages from various sources to centralized logging servers or storage systems. By using Syslog-ng, organizations can define flexible log routing and filtering rules based on message content, source, or severity level, enabling precise control over log data processing and storage. Additionally, Syslog-ng supports secure log transport protocols like TLS and SSL, ensuring data confidentiality and integrity during log transmission.

bashCopy code

```
datadog-agent run
```

This command starts the Datadog agent, enabling organizations to collect and forward log data from servers, containers, and cloud platforms to the Datadog platform for centralized storage and analysis. By using the Datadog agent, organizations can monitor log files, system logs, and application logs in real-time, extract relevant log events, and visualize them in customizable dashboards and reports. Additionally, Datadog supports log correlation and anomaly detection features, enabling organizations to identify and mitigate security threats and operational issues effectively.

In summary, centralized logging solutions play a crucial role in modern IT operations by enabling organizations to aggregate, store, and analyze log data from various sources in a centralized location. By leveraging centralized logging solutions, organizations can gain visibility into their infrastructure, detect and respond to issues proactively, and ensure the security, reliability, and compliance of their systems. Whether organizations choose open-source tools like Rsyslog, Fluentd, and Logstash, or commercial solutions like Splunk, Datadog, and Elasticsearch, implementing a centralized logging strategy is essential for maintaining the health and performance of modern IT environments.

Chapter 8: Advanced Docker Networking with Overlay Networks

In Docker, network drivers play a crucial role in enabling communication between containers and connecting containers to external networks. Understanding Docker network drivers is essential for optimizing network performance, implementing network security, and troubleshooting network-related issues in containerized environments. Docker provides several built-in network drivers, each designed to cater to specific use cases and requirements. By delving into the intricacies of Docker network drivers, operators can effectively manage container networking and ensure the seamless operation of containerized applications.

One of the most commonly used Docker network drivers is the bridge driver, which is the default network driver for Docker containers. The bridge driver creates an internal network bridge on the Docker host, allowing containers to communicate with each other using IP addresses assigned by Docker's built-in DHCP server. To create a bridge network in Docker, operators can use the following command:

bashCopy code

```
docker network create <network-name>
```

This command creates a new bridge network in Docker with the specified name, enabling containers to communicate with each other over the internal network bridge. Bridge networks are suitable for single-host deployments and are ideal for isolating containers from external networks while enabling inter-container communication.

Another widely used Docker network driver is the host driver, which allows containers to share the network namespace with the Docker host. Unlike the bridge driver, which creates a separate network namespace for each container, the host driver eliminates the overhead of network address translation (NAT) by directly exposing container ports to the host's network interface. To create a host network in Docker, operators can use the following command:

bashCopy code

```
docker run --network host <image-name>
```

This command runs a Docker container using the host network mode, enabling the container to use the host's network stack and share the host's network interfaces. Host networks are suitable for high-performance applications that require direct access to the host's network resources, such as database servers or network-intensive workloads.

In addition to bridge and host networks, Docker also supports overlay networks, which enable communication between containers running on different Docker hosts or across multiple Docker Swarm nodes. Overlay networks use the VXLAN (Virtual Extensible LAN) protocol to encapsulate and route container traffic between nodes, providing a secure and scalable networking solution for distributed applications. To create an overlay network in Docker Swarm, operators can use the following command:

bashCopy code

```
docker network create --driver overlay <network-name>
```

This command creates a new overlay network in Docker Swarm with the specified name, enabling containers to communicate securely across multiple Docker Swarm nodes. Overlay networks are ideal for deploying microservices architectures and distributed applications that require seamless communication between containers running on different hosts.

Furthermore, Docker provides the macvlan network driver, which allows containers to have their own MAC addresses and appear as physical devices on the host's network. This enables containers to communicate directly with external devices on the network without any NAT overhead. To create a macvlan network in Docker, operators can use the following command:

bashCopy code

```
docker network create --driver macvlan --subnet=<subnet> --gateway=<gateway> -o parent=<interface> <network-name>
```

This command creates a new macvlan network in Docker with the specified subnet, gateway, and parent interface, enabling containers to communicate directly with external devices on the host's network. Macvlan networks are suitable for scenarios where containers need direct access to external networks, such as IoT (Internet of Things) deployments or network appliance emulation.

Additionally, Docker offers the none network driver, which disables networking for containers, allowing them to run in complete isolation from the host's network. This can be useful for running containers with limited network access or for testing purposes. To run a Docker container with no networking, operators can use the following command:

bashCopy code

```
docker run --network none <image-name>
```

This command runs a Docker container with no networking enabled, isolating the container from the host's network and preventing it from communicating with external networks. None networks are suitable for scenarios where containers do not require network access or need to be completely isolated from the host's network.

In summary, Docker network drivers are essential for enabling communication between containers, connecting containers to external networks, and ensuring the seamless operation of containerized applications. By understanding the capabilities and use cases of different Docker network drivers, operators can optimize container networking, improve network security, and troubleshoot network-related issues effectively in containerized environments.

Docker Swarm is a powerful container orchestration tool that allows users to deploy and manage containerized applications across a cluster of Docker hosts. One of the key features of Docker Swarm is its support for overlay networks, which enable communication between containers running on different hosts within the Swarm cluster. While overlay networks provide a simple and flexible way to connect containers across hosts, they are typically limited to a single subnet by default. However, in scenarios where containers need to communicate across multiple subnets, such as in geographically distributed deployments or hybrid cloud environments, implementing multi-subnet overlay networks becomes essential. By configuring multi-subnet overlay networks in Docker Swarm, users can facilitate communication between containers deployed in different subnets, enabling seamless connectivity and scalability for distributed applications.

To implement multi-subnet overlay networks in Docker Swarm, users need to define and configure overlay networks spanning across multiple subnets within their Swarm cluster. This involves creating overlay networks with different subnet configurations and ensuring proper routing between these subnets to enable communication between containers.

The first step in implementing multi-subnet overlay networks is to create overlay networks with specific subnet configurations using the Docker CLI. Users can use the **docker network create** command to create overlay networks with custom subnet settings. For example, to create an overlay network named **multi-subnet-net** with a subnet of **10.1.0.0/16**, users can use the following command:

bashCopy code

```
docker network create --driver=overlay --subnet=10.1.0.0/16 multi-subnet-net
```

This command creates an overlay network named **multi-subnet-net** with the specified subnet configuration, enabling containers to communicate within the **10.1.0.0/16** subnet across the Docker Swarm cluster.

Once overlay networks with custom subnet configurations are created, users need to ensure proper routing between these subnets to facilitate communication between containers. This involves configuring network routing within the Swarm cluster to allow traffic between containers deployed in different subnets.

In Docker Swarm, routing between overlay networks is automatically handled by the Swarm routing mesh, which uses IP encapsulation techniques to route traffic between containers across different subnets. Users do not need to manually configure routing between overlay networks, as the Swarm routing mesh dynamically routes traffic based on service discovery and load balancing.

However, users need to ensure that Docker Swarm nodes are properly configured to support multi-subnet overlay networks and that network routing rules are configured correctly to allow traffic between containers across different subnets.

Users can verify the routing configuration of Docker Swarm nodes using the Docker CLI and inspecting network settings for each node. For example, users can use the **docker node inspect** command to retrieve detailed information about a Docker Swarm node, including its network settings and routing configuration.

bashCopy code

```
docker node inspect <node-id>
```

By inspecting Docker Swarm nodes, users can ensure that network interfaces are properly configured to support multi-subnet overlay networks and that routing rules are correctly applied to enable communication between containers deployed in different subnets.

Additionally, users can deploy services and containers within the Docker Swarm cluster, specifying the appropriate overlay network to use for inter-container communication.

When deploying services or containers, users can use the **--network** flag to specify the overlay network to use for networking. For example, to deploy a service named **web** using the overlay network **multi-subnet-net**, users can use the following command:

bashCopy code

```
docker service create --name web --network multi-subnet-net nginx
```

This command creates a service named **web** using the nginx image and connects it to the **multi-subnet-net** overlay network, enabling communication between containers deployed in different subnets within the Docker Swarm cluster.

By configuring overlay networks with custom subnet configurations and ensuring proper routing between subnets, users can implement multi-subnet overlay networks in Docker Swarm, enabling seamless communication between containers deployed across different subnets within the Swarm cluster.

This allows users to deploy and scale distributed applications in geographically distributed environments or hybrid cloud infrastructures, leveraging the flexibility and scalability of Docker Swarm for container orchestration.

Chapter 9: High Availability and Disaster Recovery Strategies with Docker

High availability is a critical requirement for modern applications, ensuring continuous operation and minimal downtime. Docker Swarm, as a container orchestration tool, offers built-in support for high availability, allowing users to deploy and manage containerized applications across a cluster of Docker hosts while ensuring fault tolerance and resilience. By leveraging Docker Swarm's features and best practices, users can implement high availability architectures for their applications, ensuring seamless operation and scalability in production environments.

To implement high availability with Docker Swarm, users need to set up a Swarm cluster consisting of multiple Docker hosts, also known as Swarm nodes. These nodes work together to distribute and manage containerized applications, providing redundancy and fault tolerance to ensure continuous operation.

The first step in implementing high availability with Docker Swarm is to initialize a Swarm cluster by designating one of the Docker hosts as the Swarm manager node. This can be done using the **docker swarm init** command on the chosen manager node:

bashCopy code

```
docker swarm init --advertise-addr <manager-node-ip>
```

This command initializes a new Docker Swarm cluster on the specified manager node and generates a unique Swarm join token that can be used by other Docker hosts to join the cluster as worker nodes.

Once the Swarm manager node is initialized, users can join additional Docker hosts to the Swarm cluster as worker nodes using the Swarm join token generated during initialization. This can be done using the **docker swarm join** command on each worker node:

bashCopy code

```
docker swarm join --token <swarm-token> <manager-node-ip>:<manager-node-port>
```

This command joins the Docker host to the existing Swarm cluster as a worker node, allowing it to participate in the distributed management of containerized applications.

With the Swarm cluster set up and running, users can deploy containerized services and applications to the cluster using Docker Swarm's service abstraction. Services in Docker Swarm are scalable, distributed units of containerized applications that can be deployed across multiple nodes in the Swarm cluster.

To deploy a service to the Swarm cluster, users can use the **docker service create** command, specifying the desired number of replicas and other service parameters:

bashCopy code

```bash
docker service create --name <service-name> --replicas <num-replicas> <image-name>
```

This command creates a new service in the Swarm cluster with the specified name and number of replicas, using the specified Docker image as the application source.

One of the key features of Docker Swarm that enables high availability is automatic service failover. In the event of a node failure or other disruptions, Docker Swarm automatically reschedules failed tasks to healthy nodes in the cluster, ensuring continuous operation of containerized services.

Additionally, Docker Swarm provides built-in load balancing and service discovery capabilities, allowing incoming requests to be distributed evenly across multiple replicas of a service and enabling seamless communication between services deployed in the Swarm cluster.

To monitor the health and status of services running in the Swarm cluster, users can use the **docker service ps** command to view the running tasks and their associated containers:

bashCopy code

```bash
docker service ps <service-name>
```

This command displays detailed information about the tasks associated with the specified service, including their status, placement, and health.

In summary, implementing high availability with Docker Swarm involves setting up a Swarm cluster consisting of multiple Docker hosts, deploying containerized services to the cluster, and leveraging Swarm's built-in features for fault tolerance, scalability, and service discovery. By following best practices and utilizing Docker Swarm's capabilities, users can ensure continuous operation and resilience for their containerized applications in production environments.

Disaster recovery planning and backup strategies are crucial components of any robust IT infrastructure, ensuring business continuity and data integrity in the face of unexpected events or disasters. In the context of containerized environments managed by Docker, disaster recovery planning involves implementing strategies to protect containerized applications and data, minimize downtime, and facilitate rapid recovery in the event of a disaster or data loss scenario. Docker provides several features and tools that can be leveraged to implement effective disaster recovery and backup strategies for containerized applications, helping organizations mitigate risks and ensure the resilience of their containerized infrastructure.

One of the fundamental aspects of disaster recovery planning is regular data backups, which involve creating copies of critical data and application configurations to safeguard against data loss. In Docker environments, backing up containerized applications involves capturing the state of Docker containers, volumes, and other resources to ensure that they can be restored in the event of a disaster. Docker provides several mechanisms for backing up containerized applications, including Docker volumes, Docker Compose files, and Docker images.

To back up Docker volumes, which store persistent data used by containerized applications, users can use the **docker volume** command to create snapshots of volumes and export them to external storage or backup repositories. For example, to back up a Docker volume named **data-volume**, users can use the following command:

bashCopy code

```
docker volume create --name data-volume-backup --driver local --opt type=none --opt device=/path/to/backup docker run --rm -v data-volume:/source -v data-volume-backup:/target alpine tar -cC /source . | tar -xC /target
```

This command creates a backup volume named **data-volume-backup** and copies the contents of the **data-volume** volume to the backup volume using the **tar** command.

In addition to backing up Docker volumes, it is essential to create backups of Docker Compose files, which define the configuration and dependencies of containerized applications. Docker Compose files can be versioned using version control systems such as Git or backed up to external repositories to ensure that they can be restored in the event of a disaster. Users can use the **git** command to clone Docker Compose files from a Git repository or use file synchronization tools to replicate Compose files to backup locations.

bashCopy code

```
git clone <repository-url>
```

This command clones the Docker Compose files from the specified Git repository to the local filesystem, allowing users to maintain versioned backups of their application configurations.

Furthermore, Docker images, which serve as the building blocks for containerized applications, should be backed up regularly to ensure that they can be restored in the event of a disaster or data loss. Docker images can be pushed to Docker Hub or other container registries, allowing users to retrieve and restore them as needed. Users can use the **docker push** command to push Docker images to a registry, as shown below:

bashCopy code

```
docker push <image-name>
```

This command pushes the specified Docker image to the configured container registry, making it available for retrieval and restoration in the event of a disaster.

In addition to regular backups, disaster recovery planning also involves implementing strategies for rapid recovery and restoration of containerized applications in the event of a disaster. Docker Swarm, as a container orchestration tool, provides features such as service replication and automatic failover, which help ensure the resilience of containerized applications and facilitate rapid recovery in the event of node failures or other disruptions.

By deploying containerized applications as Docker services in a Swarm cluster with multiple nodes, users can leverage Swarm's built-in features for service replication and automatic failover to ensure continuous operation and rapid recovery in the event of a disaster. Swarm automatically redistributes failed tasks to healthy nodes in the cluster, ensuring that containerized applications remain available and responsive even in the face of node failures or other disruptions.

Furthermore, Docker Swarm provides rolling updates and rollback capabilities, allowing users to update containerized applications with minimal downtime and roll back to previous versions in the event of deployment failures or compatibility issues. Users can use the **docker service update** command to perform rolling updates of Docker services, as shown below:

bashCopy code

```
docker service update --image <new-image> <service-name>
```

This command updates the specified Docker service with a new image, triggering a rolling update that updates containers in a controlled manner to minimize downtime and ensure service availability.

In summary, disaster recovery planning and backup strategies are essential components of maintaining a resilient and reliable Docker environment. By implementing regular backups of Docker volumes,

Compose files, and images, and leveraging Docker Swarm's features for service replication, automatic failover, and rolling updates, organizations can ensure the resilience and continuity of their containerized applications in the face of disasters and unexpected events.

Chapter 10: Optimizing Docker Performance and Scalability

Optimizing the performance of Docker hosts and containers is crucial for ensuring the efficient operation of containerized applications and maximizing resource utilization in production environments. Docker provides various tools and techniques that allow users to fine-tune the performance of Docker hosts and containers, improving responsiveness, scalability, and resource efficiency. By understanding the factors that affect Docker performance and implementing best practices for performance tuning, users can achieve optimal performance and scalability for their containerized applications.

One of the key factors that affect Docker performance is the configuration of Docker hosts, including resource allocation, kernel settings, and networking configurations. Docker hosts should be provisioned with an adequate amount of CPU, memory, and storage resources to support the workload requirements of containerized applications. Users can use the **docker info** command to view detailed information about the resources and configuration of Docker hosts:

bashCopy code

```
docker info
```

This command displays information about the Docker daemon, including the operating system, kernel version, CPU architecture, memory and storage configuration, and networking settings. Users can use this information to assess the resource utilization of Docker hosts and identify potential bottlenecks or areas for optimization.

In addition to resource allocation, optimizing kernel settings can significantly improve the performance of Docker hosts and containers. Users can adjust kernel parameters such as file descriptor limits, network buffer sizes, and process scheduling policies to optimize the performance of containerized applications. Kernel parameters can be modified using the **sysctl** command, as shown below:

bashCopy code

```
sysctl -w <parameter>=<value>
```

For example, to increase the maximum number of file descriptors allowed per process, users can use the following command:

bashCopy code

```
sysctl -w fs.file-max=100000
```

This command sets the maximum number of file descriptors to 100,000, allowing containerized applications to open more files concurrently and improve performance.

Furthermore, optimizing Docker networking can significantly impact the performance of containerized applications, especially in environments with high network traffic or latency-sensitive workloads. Docker provides several networking drivers, such as bridge, overlay, and host, each with different performance characteristics and use cases. Users can select the appropriate networking driver based on their application requirements and performance goals. Users can configure Docker networking settings using the **docker network** command, as shown below:

bashCopy code

```
docker network create --driver <driver> <network-name>
```

For example, to create an overlay network named **my-overlay-network**, users can use the following command:

bashCopy code

```
docker network create --driver overlay my-overlay-network
```

This command creates an overlay network using the overlay networking driver, which is suitable for connecting containers running on different Docker hosts in a Swarm cluster.

Another aspect of performance tuning for Docker hosts and containers is optimizing container resource allocation, including CPU, memory, and I/O resources. Docker provides several mechanisms for controlling resource allocation, such as CPU shares, memory limits, and I/O bandwidth constraints. Users can specify resource limits and constraints when creating or updating Docker containers using the **docker run** or **docker update** commands, as shown below:

bashCopy code

```
docker run --cpu-shares <shares> --memory <memory-limit> --cpus <cpu-limit> <image-name>
```

This command creates a new Docker container with specified CPU shares, memory limit, and CPU limit, ensuring that the container is allocated the appropriate amount of resources to meet its workload requirements.

Additionally, users can monitor and analyze the performance of Docker hosts and containers using monitoring tools such as Prometheus, Grafana, and Docker Stats. These tools provide insights into resource utilization, performance metrics, and container health, allowing users to identify performance bottlenecks, troubleshoot issues, and optimize resource allocation. Users can deploy monitoring tools as Docker containers and configure them to collect and visualize performance metrics from Docker hosts and containers.

In summary, performance tuning for Docker hosts and containers is essential for achieving optimal performance, scalability, and resource efficiency in containerized environments. By optimizing Docker host configuration, kernel settings, networking configurations, and container resource allocation, users can maximize the performance of their containerized applications and ensure efficient resource utilization. Additionally, monitoring and analyzing performance metrics using monitoring tools allow users to identify performance bottlenecks and optimize resource allocation for improved performance and scalability.

Scaling techniques are essential for managing the performance, availability, and resilience of applications deployed in containerized environments. Horizontal and vertical scaling are two common approaches used to scale containerized applications, each offering unique advantages and considerations. Horizontal scaling involves adding more instances of an application across multiple containers or nodes, while vertical scaling involves increasing the resources allocated to individual containers or nodes. By understanding these scaling techniques and their implications, users can effectively scale their containerized applications to meet varying workload demands and performance requirements.

Horizontal scaling, also known as scale-out scaling, involves increasing the number of instances or replicas of an application to distribute the workload across multiple containers or nodes. This approach is particularly suitable for applications that are stateless or can be easily distributed across multiple instances without requiring shared state or coordination. Docker Swarm and Kubernetes, two popular container orchestration platforms, support horizontal scaling through the use of replica sets or deployment replicas, allowing users to scale applications horizontally based on predefined criteria such as CPU utilization, memory consumption, or request throughput.

In Docker Swarm, users can scale services horizontally using the **docker service scale** command, specifying the desired number of replicas for the service. For example, to scale a service named **web** to five replicas, users can use the following command:

bashCopy code

```
docker service scale web=5
```

This command scales the **web** service to five replicas, distributing the workload across multiple containers running on different Docker Swarm nodes.

Similarly, in Kubernetes, users can scale deployments horizontally using the **kubectl scale** command, specifying the desired number of replicas for the deployment. For example, to scale a deployment named **app** to three replicas, users can use the following command:

bashCopy code

```
kubectl scale deployment app --replicas=3
```

This command scales the **app** deployment to three replicas, ensuring high availability and load distribution across multiple pods running on different Kubernetes nodes.

Horizontal scaling offers several benefits, including improved availability, fault tolerance, and scalability. By distributing the workload across multiple instances or replicas, horizontal scaling helps prevent single points of failure and ensures that applications can handle increased traffic or workload demands without sacrificing performance or responsiveness.

Additionally, horizontal scaling enables seamless deployment and scaling of containerized applications in dynamic and elastic environments, allowing users to respond quickly to changes in workload or demand. Vertical scaling, on the other hand, involves increasing the resources allocated to individual containers or nodes to handle increased workload demands or resource-intensive tasks. This approach is particularly suitable for applications that require more CPU, memory, or storage resources to meet performance requirements or process larger datasets. Docker provides several mechanisms for vertical scaling, including adjusting container resource limits, upgrading host hardware, or using container orchestration platforms with support for dynamic resource allocation and scaling.

In Docker, users can vertically scale containers by adjusting resource limits such as CPU shares, memory limits, and I/O constraints using the **docker run** or **docker update** commands. For example, to create a container with a memory limit of 2GB and two CPU cores, users can use the following command:

bashCopy code

```
docker run --memory 2g --cpus 2 <image-name>
```

This command creates a new Docker container with specified memory and CPU limits, ensuring that the container is allocated the necessary resources to meet its workload requirements.

Vertical scaling offers several advantages, including simplified management, reduced overhead, and improved resource utilization. By increasing the resources allocated to individual containers or nodes, vertical scaling helps optimize resource usage and improve performance for resource-intensive applications or tasks. Additionally, vertical scaling can be more cost-effective than horizontal scaling for applications with low or predictable workload demands, as it eliminates the overhead of managing and maintaining multiple instances or replicas.

In summary, horizontal and vertical scaling are two essential techniques used to scale containerized applications in production environments. Horizontal scaling involves adding more instances or replicas of an application to distribute the workload across multiple containers or nodes, while vertical scaling involves increasing the resources allocated to individual containers or nodes. By understanding the benefits and considerations of each scaling technique, users can effectively scale their containerized applications to meet varying workload demands, improve performance, and ensure high availability and resilience.

BOOK 3

DOCKER DEPLOYMENT STRATEGIES
SCALING AND ORCHESTRATING CONTAINERS

ROB BOTWRIGHT

Chapter 1: Introduction to Docker Deployment Strategies

Deploying applications is a critical aspect of software development and operations, with various approaches available to meet different requirements and scenarios. Each deployment approach offers distinct advantages and considerations, ranging from simplicity and flexibility to scalability and resilience. By understanding the characteristics and use cases of different deployment approaches, users can choose the most suitable method for their applications and infrastructure needs.

One common deployment approach is the traditional on-premises deployment model, where applications are deployed and managed on servers located within an organization's data center or physical infrastructure. In this model, applications are typically installed directly on physical or virtual servers, with manual configuration and management processes. While on-premises deployment offers full control over hardware and software environments, it can be complex and time-consuming to manage, requiring expertise in server administration and infrastructure provisioning.

To deploy applications on-premises, users can use configuration management tools such as Ansible, Puppet, or Chef to automate the provisioning and configuration of servers and software components.

These tools allow users to define infrastructure as code and deploy applications consistently across multiple environments, reducing manual effort and ensuring reproducibility. For example, with Ansible, users can define deployment playbooks to install and configure applications on target servers using YAML-based configuration files.

bashCopy code

```
ansible-playbook deploy.yml
```

This command executes the Ansible playbook named **deploy.yml**, which contains tasks for deploying and configuring applications on target servers according to the defined specifications.

Another deployment approach is cloud-based deployment, where applications are deployed and hosted on cloud infrastructure provided by third-party cloud service providers such as Amazon Web Services (AWS), Microsoft Azure, or Google Cloud Platform (GCP). Cloud-based deployment offers scalability, elasticity, and cost-efficiency, allowing users to deploy and scale applications dynamically based on demand.

To deploy applications on cloud infrastructure, users can use cloud-native deployment tools and services such as AWS Elastic Beanstalk, Azure App Service, or Google Kubernetes Engine (GKE). These platforms provide managed services for deploying, scaling, and managing applications in the cloud, abstracting away the underlying infrastructure complexity. For example, with AWS Elastic Beanstalk, users can deploy applications by uploading application code or

Docker containers to the Elastic Beanstalk environment and letting the platform handle deployment and scaling automatically.

bashCopy code

```
eb deploy
```

This command deploys the application to AWS Elastic Beanstalk using the configured deployment settings and environment configuration.

Containerized deployment is another popular approach for deploying applications, where applications are packaged as lightweight, portable containers and deployed across different environments consistently. Containers encapsulate application code, dependencies, and runtime environments, allowing for seamless deployment and scalability across diverse infrastructure environments.

To deploy applications using containers, users can use container orchestration platforms such as Docker Swarm, Kubernetes, or Amazon ECS (Elastic Container Service). These platforms provide tools and services for managing containerized applications at scale, including deployment, scaling, service discovery, and load balancing. For example, with Kubernetes, users can define deployment manifests or Helm charts to specify the desired state of their applications and deploy them to Kubernetes clusters.

bashCopy code

```
kubectl apply -f deployment.yaml
```

This command applies the deployment manifest specified in the **deployment.yaml** file to the

Kubernetes cluster, creating and managing application deployments according to the defined specifications.

Serverless deployment is an emerging deployment approach where applications are deployed and run as individual functions or services without the need to manage underlying infrastructure. Serverless platforms such as AWS Lambda, Azure Functions, or Google Cloud Functions abstract away server management and provisioning, allowing users to focus on writing and deploying code.

To deploy applications using serverless platforms, users can define serverless functions or services and upload application code or scripts to the platform. The platform handles deployment, scaling, and execution of functions automatically, charging users based on resource consumption or invocation counts. For example, with AWS Lambda, users can create Lambda functions using supported programming languages such as Python, Node.js, or Java and deploy them using the AWS Management Console or CLI.

bashCopy code

```
aws lambda create-function --function-name my-function --runtime nodejs14.x --handler index.handler --role arn:aws:iam::123456789012:role/service-role/MyLambdaRole --code S3Bucket=my-bucket,S3Key=my-function.zip
```

This command creates a new Lambda function named **my-function** using Node.js runtime and deploys the function code stored in an S3 bucket.

In summary, understanding different deployment approaches is essential for deploying applications effectively in diverse environments and scenarios. Whether deploying on-premises, in the cloud, using containers, or serverless platforms, each approach offers unique benefits and considerations. By leveraging the appropriate deployment tools and techniques, users can deploy applications efficiently, scale dynamically, and meet evolving business requirements and customer demands.

Containerized deployments offer numerous advantages over traditional deployment methods, providing organizations with greater flexibility, efficiency, and scalability in managing their applications and infrastructure. By encapsulating applications and their dependencies into lightweight, portable containers, containerized deployments enable seamless deployment across diverse environments, improved resource utilization, and simplified management of complex applications.

One of the primary benefits of containerized deployments is enhanced consistency and portability. Containers package applications, along with their dependencies and runtime environments, into self-contained units that can run consistently across different environments, from development to production. This consistency ensures that applications behave the same way regardless of the underlying infrastructure, eliminating the "it works on my machine" problem commonly encountered in traditional deployment models.

To demonstrate the portability of containerized deployments, organizations can use container orchestration platforms such as Docker Swarm or Kubernetes to deploy applications across multiple environments seamlessly. Using the Docker CLI, developers can create Docker images containing their applications and deploy them to any environment that supports Docker containers. For example, to build a Docker image for a web application and deploy it to a Kubernetes cluster, developers can use the following commands:

bashCopy code

```
docker build -t my-web-app . docker tag my-web-app gcr.io/my-project/my-web-app:v1 docker push gcr.io/my-project/my-web-app:v1 kubectl create deployment my-web-app --image=gcr.io/my-project/my-web-app:v1
```

These commands build a Docker image for the web application, tag it with a version identifier, push it to a container registry, and deploy it to a Kubernetes cluster using the **kubectl create deployment** command.

Another significant benefit of containerized deployments is resource efficiency and isolation. Containers share the host operating system kernel while providing process isolation, allowing multiple containers to run on the same host without conflicts. This shared kernel approach reduces overhead compared to traditional virtualization methods, where each virtual machine requires its own operating system instance. As a result, organizations can achieve higher resource utilization and cost savings by running more applications on fewer physical or virtual servers.

To demonstrate resource efficiency with containerized deployments, organizations can use container orchestration platforms to optimize resource utilization and scale applications dynamically based on demand. Kubernetes, for example, provides features such as horizontal pod autoscaling and cluster autoscaling to automatically adjust the number of running containers or nodes based on resource usage metrics. By enabling autoscaling, organizations can ensure that applications have sufficient resources to handle fluctuating workloads while minimizing resource wastage during periods of low demand.

bashCopy code

```
kubectl autoscale deployment my-web-app --cpu-percent=80 --min=1 --max=10
```

This command configures horizontal pod autoscaling for the **my-web-app** deployment in Kubernetes, scaling the number of pod replicas between 1 and 10 based on CPU utilization, with a target CPU utilization of 80%.

Additionally, containerized deployments promote faster and more efficient development and deployment workflows through the use of container registries and continuous integration/continuous deployment (CI/CD) pipelines. By storing container images in registries such as Docker Hub or Google Container Registry, organizations can version control their application artifacts and easily share them across development teams and environments. CI/CD pipelines automate the build, test, and deployment process, enabling organizations to deliver updates and new features to production faster and with greater confidence.

To illustrate CI/CD workflows with containerized deployments, organizations can use CI/CD tools such as Jenkins, GitLab CI/CD, or GitHub Actions to automate the deployment of containerized applications. These tools integrate with container registries and container orchestration platforms to build Docker images, run tests, and deploy applications automatically based on predefined triggers or schedules. For example, a Jenkins pipeline script might include stages for building Docker images, running unit tests, and deploying applications to Kubernetes clusters:

groovyCopy code

```
pipeline { agent any stages { stage('Build') { steps { sh
'docker build -t my-web-app .' } } stage('Test') { steps {
```

// Run unit tests } } stage('Deploy') { steps { sh 'kubectl apply -f deployment.yaml' } } } }

This Jenkins pipeline script defines stages for building the Docker image, running tests, and deploying the application using Kubernetes manifests.

In summary, containerized deployments offer numerous benefits for organizations looking to modernize their application deployment processes and infrastructure. From enhanced consistency and portability to resource efficiency and streamlined development workflows, containerized deployments enable organizations to deploy and manage applications more effectively in today's dynamic and cloud-native environments. By adopting containerization and container orchestration technologies, organizations can unlock the full potential of containerized deployments and accelerate their digital transformation journey.

Chapter 2: Scalable Architectures with Docker Swarm

Setting up and managing a Swarm cluster is an essential skill for deploying and orchestrating containerized applications at scale. Docker Swarm is a built-in container orchestration tool that enables users to create and manage a cluster of Docker hosts, allowing for easy deployment, scaling, and management of containerized applications across multiple nodes. By understanding the process of setting up and managing a Swarm cluster, users can leverage the power of container orchestration to streamline their application deployment workflows and improve resource utilization.

To begin setting up a Swarm cluster, the first step is to initialize the Swarm on a manager node using the **docker swarm init** command. This command initializes the Swarm cluster and generates a join token that other nodes can use to join the cluster. For example:

bashCopy code

```
docker swarm init --advertise-addr <MANAGER-IP>
```

This command initializes the Swarm cluster on the manager node and specifies the IP address to advertise to other nodes for joining the cluster.

Once the Swarm cluster is initialized, additional worker nodes can join the cluster by running the

docker swarm join command with the join token generated during initialization. For example:

bashCopy code

```
docker swarm join --token <TOKEN> <MANAGER-IP>:2377
```

This command joins the worker node to the Swarm cluster using the specified join token and the IP address of the manager node.

After setting up the Swarm cluster, users can deploy services and manage them using the Docker CLI or Docker API. Services in Swarm represent the tasks that run containers, allowing users to define desired state configurations for their applications. To deploy a service to the Swarm cluster, users can use the **docker service create** command. For example:

bashCopy code

```
docker service create --replicas 3 --name webapp nginx:latest
```

This command creates a service named **webapp** with three replicas running the **nginx:latest** image.

To view the services running in the Swarm cluster, users can use the **docker service ls** command. This command displays a list of services along with their replicas, image, and other details. For example:

bashCopy code

```
docker service ls
```

To scale a service in the Swarm cluster, users can use the **docker service scale** command. This command allows users to adjust the number of replicas for a service dynamically. For example:

bashCopy code

```
docker service scale webapp=5
```

This command scales the **webapp** service to five replicas, increasing the number of containers running the application.

In addition to deploying and managing services, Swarm clusters also support rolling updates and rollbacks for applications. Rolling updates allow users to update the configuration or image of a service without causing downtime. Users can update a service using the **docker service update** command and specify parameters such as the image to use or the number of replicas. For example:

bashCopy code

```
docker service update --image nginx:1.19.10 webapp
```

This command updates the **webapp** service to use the **nginx:1.19.10** image.

To perform a rolling update, Docker Swarm updates the service one container at a time, ensuring that the application remains available throughout the update process. If any issues arise during the update, users can rollback to a previous version of the service using the **docker service rollback** command. For example:

bashCopy code

```
docker service rollback webapp
```

This command rolls back the **webapp** service to the previous configuration, undoing any changes made during the update.

Monitoring and managing the health of services in a Swarm cluster is essential for ensuring the reliability and availability of applications. Swarm clusters include built-in support for health checks, allowing users to define checks for containers and services to monitor their status and performance. Users can specify health checks when creating or updating services using the **--health-cmd** and **--health-interval** options. For example:

bashCopy code

```
docker service create --name webapp --health-cmd="curl -f http://localhost/ || exit 1" --health-interval=5s nginx:latest
```

This command creates a service named **webapp** with a health check that runs every 5 seconds and checks the availability of the application by sending a request to **http://localhost/**.

In summary, setting up and managing a Swarm cluster enables users to deploy and orchestrate containerized applications efficiently. By initializing the Swarm cluster, joining worker nodes, deploying services, and managing updates and health checks, users can leverage the power of container orchestration to streamline their application deployment workflows and improve the reliability and scalability of their applications. With Docker Swarm, users can build and manage resilient and scalable infrastructure for their containerized applications with ease.

Scaling applications is a crucial aspect of modern software development, allowing organizations to meet increasing demand, improve performance, and maintain high availability. Docker Swarm, a built-in container orchestration tool in Docker, provides powerful features for scaling applications across a cluster of Docker hosts. By leveraging Swarm's capabilities, users can effortlessly scale their applications horizontally, ensuring they can handle fluctuations in workload effectively.

The process of scaling applications with Docker Swarm begins by deploying services to the Swarm cluster. A service in Docker Swarm represents the desired state of an application, defining how many instances, or replicas, of the application should run across the cluster. Users can deploy services using the **docker service create** command, specifying the desired number of replicas and other configuration options. For instance:

bashCopy code

```
docker service create --replicas 3 --name my-service
my-image:latest
```

This command creates a service named **my-service** with three replicas, each running the **my-image:latest** Docker image.

Once the service is deployed, users can monitor its performance and adjust the number of replicas as needed. Docker Swarm provides built-in support for scaling services dynamically, allowing users to increase or decrease the number of replicas based on factors such as resource utilization and incoming traffic. To scale a service in Docker Swarm, users can use the **docker service scale** command, specifying the desired number of replicas. For example:

bashCopy code

```
docker service scale my-service=5
```

This command scales the **my-service** service to five replicas, distributing the workload across additional containers to handle increased demand.

Docker Swarm employs a decentralized architecture, distributing service tasks (containers) across multiple nodes in the cluster. This distributed approach ensures high availability and fault tolerance, as services continue to operate even if individual nodes fail. When scaling applications with Docker Swarm, users can add additional worker nodes to the cluster to increase its capacity and distribute the workload more effectively. To add a new worker node to a Docker Swarm cluster, users can use the **docker swarm join** command on the node to join the existing cluster. For example:

bashCopy code

```
docker swarm join --token <TOKEN> <MANAGER-IP>:2377
```

This command instructs the node to join the Swarm cluster using the join token provided by the manager node.

Scaling applications with Docker Swarm also involves optimizing resource allocation and load balancing to ensure efficient use of cluster resources. Docker Swarm provides built-in load balancing capabilities, automatically distributing incoming requests across service replicas running on different nodes in the cluster. This load balancing mechanism helps evenly distribute traffic and prevent individual nodes from becoming overloaded. Additionally, Docker Swarm supports placement constraints and filters, allowing users to control where service tasks are deployed within the cluster based on factors such as node labels, resource availability, and geographic location.

To demonstrate the scaling capabilities of Docker Swarm, consider a scenario where an e-commerce application experiences a surge in traffic during a flash sale event. By monitoring the application's performance metrics using tools like Prometheus or Grafana, operators can detect the increase in traffic and scale the corresponding services dynamically to handle the load. Using Docker Swarm commands, operators can scale the relevant services to meet the increased demand, ensuring a seamless shopping experience for customers without compromising performance or reliability.

In summary, scaling applications with Docker Swarm offers organizations a flexible and scalable solution for managing containerized workloads across distributed environments. By leveraging Docker Swarm's built-in features for service deployment, scaling, and load balancing, users can ensure their applications can handle fluctuations in workload effectively while maintaining high availability and performance. Whether deploying microservices architectures, web applications, or batch processing workloads, Docker Swarm provides a robust platform for scaling applications and meeting the evolving needs of modern IT infrastructures.

Chapter 3: Introduction to Kubernetes for Container Orchestration

Kubernetes, often abbreviated as K8s, is an open-source container orchestration platform designed to automate the deployment, scaling, and management of containerized applications. At its core, Kubernetes operates on the principles of declarative configuration and a container-centric infrastructure, providing a robust framework for building, deploying, and scaling applications in distributed environments.

One of the fundamental concepts in Kubernetes is the idea of a cluster, which consists of a collection of nodes that collectively run containerized applications. A Kubernetes cluster typically comprises one or more master nodes and multiple worker nodes. The master node is responsible for managing the overall state of the cluster, scheduling application workloads, and orchestrating communication between nodes. Worker nodes, on the other hand, are responsible for running containerized applications and executing tasks assigned to them by the master node.

To create a Kubernetes cluster, users can leverage various deployment options, including managed Kubernetes services provided by cloud providers such as Amazon EKS, Google Kubernetes Engine (GKE), and Azure Kubernetes Service (AKS), or by deploying Kubernetes manually using tools like kubeadm, kops, or kubespray. For instance, to create a Kubernetes cluster using kubeadm, users can run the following commands:

bashCopy code

```bash
kubeadm init
```

This command initializes a new Kubernetes cluster with default configuration settings on the current node.

Once the Kubernetes cluster is up and running, users interact with it using the Kubernetes API, which serves as the primary interface for managing cluster resources. Kubernetes organizes resources into various abstractions, with each abstraction representing a different aspect of the application or infrastructure. Some of the key resources in Kubernetes include Pods, Deployments, Services, ConfigMaps, and Secrets.

Pods are the smallest deployable units in Kubernetes and represent one or more containers that share the same network namespace and storage volumes. Deployments are a higher-level abstraction that defines the desired state for managing Pods, allowing users to declaratively specify how many replicas of a Pod should be running and how they should be updated over time. Services provide a stable endpoint for accessing a set of Pods, enabling load balancing and service discovery within the cluster.

ConfigMaps and Secrets are Kubernetes resources used for managing configuration data and sensitive information, respectively. ConfigMaps store configuration settings as key-value pairs, which can be mounted as volumes or exposed as environment variables in Pods. Secrets, on the other hand, are used to store sensitive data such as passwords, API keys, and TLS certificates, with encryption at rest and in transit.

Another important concept in Kubernetes is the notion of labels and selectors, which are key-value pairs attached to Kubernetes resources for identifying and grouping related objects. Labels allow users to apply arbitrary metadata to resources, enabling dynamic selection and filtering based on specific criteria. Selectors, on the other hand, are used to query and filter resources based on their labels, facilitating operations such as service discovery, load balancing, and resource allocation.

Kubernetes also introduces the concept of controllers, which are control loops that continuously monitor the state of cluster resources and reconcile them with the desired state specified by users. Controllers play a crucial role in maintaining the desired state of applications, ensuring that Pods, Deployments, Services, and other resources are automatically created, updated, and deleted as needed.

One of the key components of Kubernetes architecture is the kube-apiserver, which exposes the Kubernetes API and serves as the front-end for interacting with the cluster. The kube-controller-manager and kube-scheduler are responsible for managing various controllers and scheduling Pods onto worker nodes, respectively. The kubelet, running on each worker node, is responsible for managing containers, executing Pod manifests, and reporting node status to the master node.

Other essential components of Kubernetes include etcd, a distributed key-value store used for storing cluster state and configuration data; kube-proxy, a network proxy that implements service abstraction and load balancing; and kube-dns or CoreDNS, which provide DNS-based service discovery within the cluster.

In summary, Kubernetes introduces a wealth of concepts and components that collectively form the foundation for building, deploying, and managing containerized applications at scale. By understanding these key concepts, users can effectively leverage Kubernetes to automate the deployment, scaling, and management of applications in distributed environments, enabling rapid development, improved resource utilization, and increased operational efficiency.

Kubernetes has emerged as the de facto standard for container orchestration, offering a powerful platform for deploying and managing applications in a scalable, reliable, and efficient manner. Deploying applications in Kubernetes involves several steps, starting from defining the application's configuration to managing its lifecycle and ensuring high availability and resilience in production environments.

The first step in deploying an application in Kubernetes is to define its configuration using

Kubernetes manifests, which are YAML or JSON files that describe the desired state of the application's components. These manifests typically include specifications for Pods, Deployments, Services, ConfigMaps, and Secrets, among other resources. For example, to create a Deployment for a web application named **my-app**, users can create a YAML manifest file like this:

yamlCopy code

apiVersion: apps/v1 kind: Deployment metadata: name: my-app spec: replicas: 3 selector: matchLabels: app: my-app template: metadata: labels: app: my-app spec: containers: - name: my-app image: my-image:latest ports: - containerPort: 80

This manifest specifies a Deployment named **my-app** with three replicas, each running a container based on the **my-image:latest** Docker image.

Once the application's configuration is defined, users can deploy it to a Kubernetes cluster using the **kubectl apply** command, which applies the configurations specified in the manifest files to the cluster. For example:

bashCopy code

```
kubectl apply -f my-app.yaml
```

This command creates or updates the resources defined in the **my-app.yaml** manifest file, ensuring that the application is deployed according to the desired state.

After deploying the application, users can monitor its status and manage its lifecycle using various kubectl commands. For instance, to view the status of Deployments in the cluster, users can use the **kubectl get deployments** command:

bashCopy code

```
kubectl get deployments
```

This command displays a list of Deployments in the cluster along with their current status, including the number of replicas desired, available, and ready.

To manage the lifecycle of the application, users can perform actions such as scaling, updating, and deleting Deployments using kubectl commands. For example, to scale the **my-app** Deployment to five replicas, users can use the **kubectl scale** command:

bashCopy code

```
kubectl scale deployment my-app --replicas=5
```

This command scales the **my-app** Deployment to five replicas, distributing the workload across additional Pods to handle increased demand.

Updating an application in Kubernetes involves modifying the configuration of its Deployments and applying the changes to the cluster. Users can update Deployments using the **kubectl apply** command with the updated manifest file. For instance, to update the image version of the **my-app** Deployment to **v2**, users can edit the **my-app.yaml** file and apply the changes:

bashCopy code

```
kubectl apply -f my-app.yaml
```

This command updates the **my-app** Deployment with the new image version, triggering a rolling update to replace existing Pods with Pods running the updated image.

In addition to deploying and managing individual applications, Kubernetes provides features for managing application configuration and secrets, exposing applications externally, and monitoring application performance and health. Kubernetes ConfigMaps and Secrets enable users to manage configuration data and sensitive information such as passwords and API keys, respectively, and inject them into application containers as environment variables or mounted volumes. To expose applications externally and enable external access, Kubernetes provides the concept of Services, which provide a stable endpoint for accessing a set of Pods. Users can create Services using YAML manifest files or the **kubectl expose** command, specifying the type of Service (e.g., ClusterIP, NodePort, or LoadBalancer) and the target Deployment or Pod.

bashCopy code

```
kubectl expose deployment my-app --type=LoadBalancer --port=80 --target-port=8080
```

This command exposes the **my-app** Deployment externally using a LoadBalancer Service, enabling external access to the application on port 80.

For monitoring application performance and health, Kubernetes integrates with various monitoring and logging solutions such as Prometheus, Grafana, and

Fluentd. Users can deploy these solutions to the cluster and configure them to collect metrics, monitor resource usage, and analyze application logs, providing insights into application behavior and performance.

Overall, deploying and managing applications in Kubernetes involves defining the application's configuration, deploying it to the cluster, monitoring its status and performance, and managing its lifecycle using kubectl commands and Kubernetes resources. By leveraging Kubernetes' powerful features for container orchestration and management, users can deploy applications with confidence, ensuring scalability, reliability, and efficiency in production environments.

Chapter 4: Deploying Applications with Docker Compose

Compose files are a powerful tool for defining and managing multi-container applications in Docker environments. These YAML-formatted files allow developers to specify the services, networks, volumes, and other configurations required to run complex applications consisting of multiple interconnected containers. Writing effective Compose files involves understanding the structure and syntax of the files, defining the services and their dependencies, configuring networking and storage, and optimizing the deployment for efficiency and scalability.

The first step in writing a Compose file for a multi-container application is to define the services that make up the application. Services represent the individual components of the application, such as web servers, databases, message brokers, and background workers. Each service is defined with its own configuration settings, including the Docker image to use, environment variables, ports to expose, volumes to mount, and dependencies on other services.

For example, consider a simple web application consisting of a web server and a database. The Compose file for this application might look like this:

yamlCopy code

version: '3' services: web: image: nginx:latest ports: - "80:80" db: image: mysql:latest environment: MYSQL_ROOT_PASSWORD: secret

In this example, the Compose file defines two services: **web** and **db**. The **web** service uses the **nginx:latest** Docker image and exposes port 80 on the host machine, while the **db** service uses the **mysql:latest** Docker image and sets the **MYSQL_ROOT_PASSWORD** environment variable to "secret".

Once the services are defined, developers can specify additional configurations such as volumes, networks, and environment variables to customize the behavior of the application. Volumes are used to persist data generated by containers, such as database files, log files, and configuration files. Networks define how containers communicate with each other and with external systems, allowing developers to isolate services and control network traffic.

For example, to configure a volume for the database service and create a custom network for the application, developers can extend the Compose file as follows:

yamlCopy code

version: '3' services: web: image: nginx:latest ports: - "80:80" networks: - mynetwork db: image: mysql:latest environment: MYSQL_ROOT_PASSWORD: secret volumes: - dbdata:/var/lib/mysql networks: - mynetwork networks: mynetwork: volumes: dbdata:

In this example, a custom network named **mynetwork** is defined at the top level of the Compose file, and both services are configured to use this network. Additionally, a volume named **dbdata** is defined to persist the database data on the host machine.

Writing Compose files for multi-container applications also involves considering best practices for optimization, scalability, and maintainability. For example, developers can leverage Docker's built-in health checks and restart policies to improve the reliability of their applications. Health checks allow containers to report their health status to Docker, enabling Docker to automatically restart unhealthy containers based on predefined criteria.

To configure a health check for a service in a Compose file, developers can use the **healthcheck** directive:

yamlCopy code

version: '3' services: web: image: nginx:latest ports: - "80:80" healthcheck: test: ["CMD", "curl", "-f", "http://localhost"] interval: 10s timeout: 5s retries: 3

In this example, the **web** service is configured with a health check that runs the command **curl -f http://localhost** every 10 seconds. If the command fails to return successfully within 5 seconds, Docker will consider the container unhealthy and attempt to restart it.

Another best practice for writing Compose files is to use environment variables for configuration instead of hardcoding values in the file. This allows developers to customize the behavior of their applications without modifying the Compose file itself, making it easier to deploy the same application in different environments.

For example, developers can define environment variables for database connection settings in the Compose file and pass them to the database service using the **environment** directive:

yamlCopy code

version: '3' services: web: image: nginx:latest ports: - "80:80" environment: DB_HOST: db DB_USER: myuser DB_PASSWORD: mypassword db: image: mysql:latest environment: MYSQL_ROOT_PASSWORD: secret

In this example, the **web** service is configured with environment variables for the database host, username, and password. These values are passed to the **db** service using Docker's built-in service discovery mechanism, allowing the web server to connect to the database without hardcoding the database connection settings.

Overall, writing Compose files for multi-container applications involves defining the services, networks, volumes, and other configurations required to run the application effectively. By understanding the structure and syntax of Compose files and following best practices for optimization and maintainability, developers can create reliable and scalable deployments for their Dockerized applications.

Deploying and managing applications with Docker Compose is a fundamental aspect of containerized development, enabling developers to define and orchestrate multi-container applications with ease. Docker Compose simplifies the process of managing complex application environments by allowing developers to define the entire application stack in a single YAML configuration file. This file, typically named **docker-compose.yml**, serves as a blueprint for the entire application infrastructure, including services, networks, volumes, and other dependencies.
To begin deploying an application with Docker Compose, developers first need to define the services that make up their application. Services represent the individual components of the application, such as web servers, databases, message brokers, and background workers. Each service is defined with its own configuration settings, including the Docker image to use, environment variables, ports to expose, volumes to mount, and dependencies on other services.
For example, to deploy a simple web application consisting of an Nginx web server and a MySQL database, developers can define the services in a **docker-compose.yml** file as follows:
yamlCopy code
version: '3' services: web: image: nginx:latest ports: - "80:80" db: image: mysql:latest environment: MYSQL_ROOT_PASSWORD: password

In this example, the **docker-compose.yml** file defines two services: **web** and **db**. The **web** service uses the **nginx:latest** Docker image and exposes port 80 on the host machine, while the **db** service uses the **mysql:latest** Docker image and sets the **MYSQL_ROOT_PASSWORD** environment variable to "password".

Once the services are defined in the **docker-compose.yml** file, developers can deploy the application using the **docker-compose up** command. This command reads the **docker-compose.yml** file, creates the necessary Docker containers, and starts the application stack. If the images specified in the **docker-compose.yml** file are not already present on the local machine, Docker Compose will automatically pull them from Docker Hub before starting the containers.

bashCopy code

```
docker-compose up
```

By default, Docker Compose will run the application in the foreground, streaming the logs of all the containers to the terminal. To run the application in the background, developers can use the **-d** or **--detach** flag:

bashCopy code

```
docker-compose up -d
```

Once the application is running, developers can use the **docker-compose ps** command to view the status of all the services in the application stack:

bashCopy code

```
docker-compose ps
```

This command provides information about the running containers, including their names, status, and exposed ports. Developers can also use the **docker-compose logs** command to view the logs of specific services in the application stack:

bashCopy code

```
docker-compose logs web
```

In addition to deploying applications, Docker Compose also provides commands for managing the application lifecycle, such as stopping and removing containers. To stop the application and shut down all the containers, developers can use the **docker-compose down** command:

bashCopy code

```
docker-compose down
```

This command stops all the containers defined in the **docker-compose.yml** file and removes them, along with any associated networks and volumes. If developers only want to stop the containers without removing them, they can use the **docker-compose stop** command:

bashCopy code

```
docker-compose stop
```

Overall, deploying and managing applications with Docker Compose streamlines the development and deployment process by providing a simple and consistent way to define, orchestrate, and manage multi-container applications. By leveraging the power of Docker Compose, developers can easily deploy complex application environments, test changes locally, and streamline their development workflows.

Chapter 5: Load Balancing and Service Discovery in Docker Environments

Implementing load balancing with Docker is essential for distributing incoming traffic across multiple containers to ensure optimal performance, scalability, and reliability of applications. One of the widely used tools for load balancing in Docker environments is Docker's built-in support for container networking, which provides various options for load balancing traffic to containers.

Docker Swarm, Docker's native clustering and orchestration tool, offers built-in load balancing capabilities through its ingress routing mesh. This routing mesh enables transparent load balancing of incoming traffic to services running in a Docker Swarm cluster. To utilize this feature, developers need to deploy their services as part of a Docker Swarm cluster and enable ingress routing.

To deploy a service as part of a Docker Swarm cluster, developers first need to initialize a Swarm on their Docker hosts using the **docker swarm init** command:

bashCopy code

```
docker swarm init
```

Once the Swarm is initialized, developers can deploy their services using Docker Swarm's service abstraction. When deploying a service, developers can specify the desired number of replicas for the service, and Docker Swarm automatically distributes the replicas across the nodes in the cluster. For example, to deploy a web service with three replicas:

bashCopy code

```
docker service create --replicas 3 --name my-web-service my-web-image
```

With the services deployed in the Swarm cluster, Docker automatically load balances incoming traffic to the replicas of the service. The ingress routing mesh handles the routing of incoming requests to the appropriate service replicas, distributing the load evenly across the nodes in the Swarm cluster.

Another option for load balancing in Docker environments is to use external load balancers in conjunction with Docker containers. External load balancers, such as NGINX or HAProxy, can be deployed as separate containers alongside application containers and configured to distribute traffic to the backend containers based on predefined rules.

To deploy an external load balancer alongside application containers, developers can use Docker Compose to define the services and their configurations in a **docker-compose.yml** file. For example, to deploy NGINX as a load balancer for a web application:

yamlCopy code

```
version: '3' services: nginx: image: nginx:latest ports: - "80:80" volumes: -
```

./nginx.conf:/etc/nginx/nginx.conf depends_on: - web web: image: my-web-image

In this example, the **nginx** service is configured to listen on port 80 and forward requests to the **web** service, which represents the application containers. Developers can customize the NGINX configuration by mounting a custom **nginx.conf** file into the container.

Once the **docker-compose.yml** file is defined, developers can deploy the services using the **docker-compose up** command:

bashCopy code

```
docker-compose up -d
```

This command starts both the NGINX load balancer and the application containers in the background, with NGINX configured to load balance incoming traffic to the application containers.

In addition to Docker Swarm and external load balancers, developers can also use container orchestration platforms like Kubernetes for advanced load balancing capabilities. Kubernetes provides built-in support for load balancing through its service abstraction, which automatically distributes traffic to pods based on predefined rules and policies.

Overall, implementing load balancing with Docker is crucial for optimizing the performance and reliability of containerized applications. Whether using Docker Swarm, external load balancers, or container orchestration platforms like Kubernetes, load balancing ensures efficient distribution of traffic across containers, enabling applications to handle high loads and scale dynamically as needed.

Service discovery in Docker environments is critical for enabling communication between containers and ensuring seamless connectivity within distributed applications. Docker offers several service discovery options, each with its own advantages and use cases. One of the primary methods for service discovery in Docker is through Docker's built-in DNS resolution mechanism.

When containers are deployed within the same Docker network, Docker automatically provides DNS resolution for container-to-container communication using container names as hostnames. This means that containers can communicate with each other using the container names as domain names, without the need for manual IP address management or configuration.

For example, if there are two containers named **web** and **db** deployed within the same Docker network, the **web** container can communicate with the **db** container using the hostname **db**. Docker's DNS resolver automatically translates the hostname **db** to the IP address of the **db** container, enabling seamless communication between the two containers.

bashCopy code

docker network create my-network docker run -d --name db --network my-network db-image docker run -d --name web --network my-network web-image

In this example, both the **web** and **db** containers are deployed within the **my-network** Docker network. As a result, the **web** container can communicate with the **db** container using the hostname **db**, without needing to know the IP address of the **db** container.

Another service discovery option in Docker environments is the use of environment variables to pass configuration information between containers. Docker allows developers to define environment variables for containers at runtime, which can be used to pass connection details and configuration parameters to other containers.

For example, when deploying a web application container that needs to connect to a database container, developers can use environment variables to pass the database connection details to the web application container:

bashCopy code

docker run -d --name db -e MYSQL_ROOT_PASSWORD=password mysql:latest docker run -d --name web -e DB_HOST=db -e DB_USER=root -e DB_PASSWORD=password web-image

In this example, the **DB_HOST**, **DB_USER**, and **DB_PASSWORD** environment variables are passed to the **web** container, providing it with the necessary connection details to connect to the **db** container.

Additionally, Docker Swarm provides built-in service discovery and load balancing capabilities through its DNS-based service discovery mechanism. When deploying services in a Docker Swarm cluster, each service is automatically assigned a DNS name that resolves to the IP addresses of all the replicas of the service. This enables seamless communication between services running in a Docker Swarm cluster without the need for manual configuration.

bashCopy code

```
docker swarm init docker service create --name web --replicas 3 -p 80:80 web-image
```

In this example, a web service with three replicas is deployed in a Docker Swarm cluster. Docker Swarm automatically assigns a DNS name to the **web** service, which resolves to the IP addresses of all the replicas of the service. This allows clients to communicate with the **web** service using its DNS name, regardless of which replica handles the request.

Overall, service discovery in Docker environments is essential for enabling communication between containers and facilitating the dynamic scaling and orchestration of distributed applications. Whether through Docker's built-in DNS resolution mechanism, environment variables, or Docker Swarm's DNS-based service discovery, Docker provides several options for seamless service discovery and connectivity within containerized environments.

Chapter 6: Monitoring and Logging in Containerized Deployments

Monitoring containerized applications is crucial for ensuring their performance, availability, and reliability in production environments. Docker provides several tools and techniques for monitoring containerized applications, allowing developers and administrators to gain insights into the health and performance of their containers and the underlying infrastructure.

One of the fundamental tools for monitoring containerized applications is Docker's built-in support for container metrics. Docker Engine collects various metrics about containers, such as CPU usage, memory usage, network activity, and disk I/O, which can be accessed using the **docker stats** command. This command provides real-time information about resource usage for each running container, enabling developers to identify performance bottlenecks and troubleshoot issues.

bashCopy code

```
docker stats [OPTIONS] [CONTAINER...]
```

By running the **docker stats** command, developers can view a continuously updating stream of resource usage metrics for one or more containers. This allows them to monitor the resource utilization of their containers and identify any containers that may be consuming excessive resources or experiencing performance issues.

In addition to Docker's built-in container metrics, developers can use monitoring and logging solutions specifically designed for containerized environments. One popular tool for container monitoring is Prometheus, an open-source monitoring and alerting toolkit that is widely used in Kubernetes and Docker environments. Prometheus collects metrics from various sources, including Docker containers, and stores them in a time-series database for analysis and visualization.

To deploy Prometheus for monitoring Docker containers, developers can use Docker Compose to define the Prometheus service and its configuration:

yamlCopy code

```
version: '3' services: prometheus: image: prom/prometheus ports: - "9090:9090" volumes: - ./prometheus.yml:/etc/prometheus/prometheus.yml
```

In this example, a Prometheus service is defined using a Docker Compose file, with port 9090 exposed for accessing the Prometheus web interface. Additionally, a **prometheus.yml** configuration file is mounted into the Prometheus container to specify the targets from which Prometheus should collect metrics.

Once the **docker-compose.yml** file is defined, developers can deploy the Prometheus service using the **docker-compose up** command:

bashCopy code

```
docker-compose up -d
```

With Prometheus deployed, developers can configure it to scrape metrics from Docker containers using the appropriate configuration in the **prometheus.yml** file. Prometheus can collect metrics from Docker containers using Docker's remote API, allowing developers to monitor resource usage, performance metrics, and custom application metrics from their containerized applications.

Alongside monitoring, logging is another essential aspect of containerized application management. Docker provides built-in support for logging, allowing developers to centralize and aggregate logs from multiple containers using Docker's logging drivers. Docker's default logging driver, **json-file**, logs container output to JSON files on the host machine, while other logging drivers such as **syslog** and **journald** can be used to send logs to external logging systems.

To configure Docker to use a specific logging driver, developers can specify the desired logging driver when running Docker containers:

bashCopy code

```
docker run --log-driver=syslog --log-opt syslog-address=udp://logs.example.com:514 my-container
```

In this example, the **--log-driver** flag is used to specify the syslog logging driver, and the **--log-opt** flag is used to configure the syslog address to which logs should be sent. By using Docker's logging drivers, developers can centralize and manage container logs more effectively, making it easier to monitor and troubleshoot containerized applications.

Overall, monitoring containerized applications is essential for ensuring their performance, availability, and reliability in production environments. Whether using Docker's built-in container metrics, tools like Prometheus for advanced monitoring, or Docker's logging drivers for centralized logging, developers have a range of options for monitoring and managing containerized applications effectively. By implementing robust monitoring and logging solutions, developers can gain valuable insights into their containerized environments and proactively address any issues that may arise.

Setting up a robust logging infrastructure is essential for effectively monitoring and troubleshooting containerized applications in Docker environments. Docker provides various options and tools for logging, enabling developers to capture, aggregate, and analyze logs generated by containers and applications running in Docker.

One of the commonly used logging solutions in Docker environments is the Docker logging driver mechanism. Docker supports multiple logging drivers, each designed to capture container logs and send them to different logging endpoints or storage systems. One popular logging driver is the **json-file** driver, which writes container logs to JSON files on the Docker host's filesystem.

To configure Docker to use the **json-file** logging driver, developers can specify the driver when starting a container using the **--log-driver** option:

bashCopy code

```
docker run -d --log-driver json-file --name my-container my-image
```

In this example, the **json-file** logging driver is specified when starting the **my-container** container. Docker will then write the container logs to JSON files located in the default log directory on the Docker host.

While the **json-file** logging driver is suitable for basic logging needs, Docker also provides support for other logging drivers that offer more advanced features and integration options. For example, the **syslog** logging driver sends container logs to the syslog daemon on the Docker host, allowing for centralized logging management and integration with existing logging infrastructure.

To use the **syslog** logging driver, developers can specify the driver and syslog endpoint when starting a container:

bashCopy code

```
docker run -d --log-driver syslog --log-opt syslog-address=udp://<syslog-host>:514 --name my-container my-image
```

In this command, the **syslog** logging driver is configured to send container logs to the syslog daemon running on the specified **<syslog-host>** at UDP port 514.

In addition to built-in logging drivers, Docker also supports third-party logging solutions and integrations through the use of logging plugins. Logging plugins extend Docker's logging capabilities by allowing developers to integrate with external logging systems and services, such as Elasticsearch, Fluentd, or Splunk.

To use a logging plugin with Docker, developers first need to install the plugin on their Docker host. Once installed, they can configure Docker to use the plugin as the logging driver for containers:

bashCopy code

```
docker run -d --log-driver <plugin-name> --name my-container my-image
```

In this command, **<plugin-name>** refers to the name of the installed logging plugin. Docker will then use the plugin to capture and forward container logs to the configured logging endpoint.

In addition to configuring Docker logging drivers at runtime, developers can also specify default logging options in the Docker daemon configuration file (**daemon.json**). This allows for centralized management and configuration of logging settings across all containers running on the Docker host.

To configure default logging options in the Docker daemon configuration file, developers can add the desired logging driver and options under the **"log-driver"** and **"log-opts"** keys:

jsonCopy code

{ "log-driver": "json-file", "log-opts": { "max-size": "10m", "max-file": "3" } }

In this example, the Docker daemon is configured to use the **json-file** logging driver with specified options, such as maximum log file size and maximum number of log files.

Overall, setting up logging infrastructure is crucial for effectively monitoring and managing containerized applications in Docker environments. By leveraging Docker's logging drivers, plugins, and configuration options, developers can capture and analyze container logs to gain insights into application performance, troubleshoot issues, and ensure the reliability of Docker deployments.

Chapter 7: Managing Secrets and Configuration in Docker

Securing sensitive information, such as passwords, API keys, and other credentials, is crucial in any software deployment, including Docker environments. Docker provides several mechanisms for securely handling secrets, ensuring that sensitive data is protected from unauthorized access and exposure.

One of the primary methods for managing secrets in Docker is through the use of Docker secrets. Docker secrets allow developers to securely store sensitive data as files or in-memory data structures and make them available to Docker containers in a secure and controlled manner.

To create a Docker secret, developers can use the **docker secret create** command, specifying the name of the secret and providing the sensitive data:

bashCopy code

```
echo "mysecretpassword" | docker secret create my_secret -
```

In this example, a Docker secret named **my_secret** is created with the value **"mysecretpassword"**. The - symbol at the end of the command indicates that the secret data is read from standard input.

Once created, Docker secrets can be mounted into containers as files or exposed as environment variables, allowing applications running inside containers to access the sensitive data securely.

To mount a Docker secret as a file inside a container, developers can use the **--secret** option when running the container:

bashCopy code

```
docker run -d --name my_container --secret my_secret my_image
```

In this command, the Docker secret named **my_secret** is mounted as a file inside the **my_container** container.

Alternatively, developers can expose Docker secrets as environment variables within containers using the -**-env** option combined with the **--secret** option:

bashCopy code

```
docker run -d --name my_container --env SECRET_VAR_FILE=/run/secrets/my_secret --secret my_secret my_image
```

In this example, the Docker secret named **my_secret** is exposed as an environment variable named **SECRET_VAR_FILE** inside the **my_container** container.

By leveraging Docker secrets, developers can ensure that sensitive data is securely managed and accessed by containers without exposing it in plaintext or risking inadvertent exposure.

In addition to Docker secrets, Docker also provides integration with external secret management systems, such as HashiCorp Vault or AWS Secrets Manager, through the use of secret drivers. Secret drivers extend Docker's secret management capabilities by allowing developers to store secrets in external secret stores and securely access them from Docker containers.

To use an external secret management system with Docker, developers first need to install and configure the appropriate secret driver plugin. Once installed, they can create and manage secrets using the external secret management system's APIs or command-line tools.

For example, to use HashiCorp Vault as the secret management system for Docker, developers can install the Docker Vault secret plugin and configure it to communicate with their Vault server. They can then create and manage secrets in Vault and access them from Docker containers using Docker secrets commands.

bashCopy code

```
docker plugin install --grant-all-permissions hashicorp/docker-vault-plugin:latest
```

Once installed, the Docker Vault secret plugin can be used to create and manage secrets stored in Vault and accessed by Docker containers securely.

By integrating with external secret management systems, Docker enables developers to leverage the advanced security features and capabilities offered by these systems while maintaining compatibility with Docker's container orchestration and deployment workflows.

Overall, securing sensitive information in Docker environments is essential for ensuring the confidentiality and integrity of data processed and stored by containerized applications. By utilizing Docker secrets and integrating with external secret management systems, developers can implement robust security measures to protect sensitive data in Docker deployments.

Configuration management is a critical aspect of maintaining consistency, reliability, and scalability in software environments. It encompasses a set of practices, tools, and techniques aimed at managing and controlling the configuration of software systems and infrastructure components. By adopting configuration management best practices, organizations can streamline deployment processes, reduce errors, and ensure that systems are configured optimally for performance and security.

One fundamental aspect of configuration management is version control. Version control systems, such as Git, enable teams to track changes to configuration files and infrastructure code over time, facilitating collaboration, traceability, and rollback capabilities. Teams can use Git commands like **git add**, **git commit**, and **git push** to manage configuration changes effectively. By maintaining a version-controlled repository of configuration files, teams can ensure that changes are documented, reversible, and auditable.

Another essential practice in configuration management is the use of configuration management tools. Tools like Ansible, Puppet, Chef, and SaltStack automate the provisioning, configuration, and management of software and infrastructure components. These tools employ declarative or imperative approaches to define desired system states and enforce configuration consistency across multiple nodes or environments. For instance, with Ansible, users can define configuration tasks in YAML files called playbooks and execute them using the **ansible-playbook** command, ensuring that systems are configured according to predefined specifications.

Infrastructure as Code (IaC) is a core principle of modern configuration management practices. IaC involves defining and managing infrastructure resources using code, allowing for automated provisioning and configuration. Tools like Terraform and AWS CloudFormation enable users to define infrastructure resources, such as virtual machines, networks, and storage, in code files called templates. These templates can be version-controlled, tested, and deployed using command-line interfaces like the Terraform CLI (**terraform apply**) or the AWS CLI (**aws cloudformation deploy**), ensuring that infrastructure configuration is consistent, repeatable, and auditable.

Continuous Integration/Continuous Deployment (CI/CD) pipelines play a vital role in configuration management by automating the testing, validation, and deployment of configuration changes. CI/CD pipelines integrate with version control systems to automatically trigger tests and deployments whenever configuration changes are committed to the repository. Tools like Jenkins, GitLab CI/CD, and CircleCI enable organizations to define and orchestrate CI/CD pipelines, ensuring that configuration changes are validated and deployed quickly and reliably.

Configuration drift is a common challenge in configuration management, occurring when the actual configuration of a system diverges from its intended state. To mitigate configuration drift, organizations can implement configuration drift detection and remediation strategies. Configuration management tools often provide features for detecting and correcting configuration drift automatically. For example, Puppet's Puppet Enterprise solution includes Puppet Remediate, a tool for identifying and resolving configuration drift across infrastructure environments.

Configuration management best practices also encompass security considerations. Organizations should adopt principles like the principle of least privilege and implement secure configuration baselines to reduce the attack surface and mitigate security risks. Tools like the Center for Internet Security (CIS) benchmarks provide guidelines for securely configuring operating systems and software applications, helping organizations align with industry best practices and regulatory requirements.

Furthermore, organizations should implement configuration backup and recovery mechanisms to safeguard against data loss and system downtime. Regularly backing up configuration files and infrastructure code ensures that organizations can restore systems to a known good state in the event of data corruption, hardware failure, or other unforeseen incidents. CLI commands like **tar** or **rsync** can be used to create backups of configuration files and infrastructure code, while version control systems provide additional redundancy and history tracking capabilities.

In summary, configuration management best practices are essential for maintaining consistency, reliability, and security in software environments. By leveraging version control, configuration management tools, Infrastructure as Code, CI/CD pipelines, and security measures, organizations can ensure that systems are configured optimally and managed efficiently throughout their lifecycle. Implementing these best practices enables organizations to achieve greater agility, scalability, and resilience in their software deployments.

Chapter 8: Advanced Deployment Techniques: Blue-Green Deployments, Canary Releases

Blue-green deployment is a deployment strategy used to minimize downtime and risk during software releases by maintaining two identical production environments, referred to as blue and green. In this approach, only one environment, either blue or green, is active at any given time, while the other environment remains idle. The strategy involves gradually transitioning traffic from the active environment to the inactive one, allowing for seamless deployment and rollback if issues arise.

To implement blue-green deployment with Docker, organizations typically utilize container orchestration platforms like Docker Swarm or Kubernetes, which offer built-in support for managing multiple deployment environments and routing traffic between them. These platforms allow users to define services and deploy containerized applications across multiple nodes or clusters, ensuring high availability and scalability.

The first step in implementing blue-green deployment with Docker is to set up two identical environments, one serving as the blue environment and the other as the green environment. Each environment consists of a set of Docker containers running the application and any required dependencies. CLI commands like

docker stack deploy in Docker Swarm or **kubectl apply** in Kubernetes can be used to deploy application services to each environment.

Once the blue and green environments are set up, traffic routing mechanisms are configured to direct user requests to the active environment. In Docker Swarm, this can be achieved using ingress routing or service discovery mechanisms like Docker's built-in DNS resolution. Similarly, Kubernetes uses services and ingress resources to manage traffic routing between pods and services.

Before transitioning traffic to the green environment, the new version of the application is deployed and tested in isolation to ensure that it functions correctly. This can be done by updating the Docker image tag or version number in the deployment configuration files and deploying the updated configuration to the green environment using CLI commands like **docker service update** or **kubectl apply**.

Once the new version of the application is deployed to the green environment and passes testing, traffic routing mechanisms are updated to gradually shift incoming requests from the blue environment to the green environment. This can be achieved by updating DNS records, load balancer configurations, or service endpoints to point to the green environment gradually. In Docker Swarm, rolling updates can be performed using commands like **docker service**

update --image to update the service to the new version gradually.

During the transition process, monitoring and logging tools are used to monitor the health and performance of the application in real-time. This allows organizations to detect any issues or anomalies and roll back the deployment if necessary. Docker provides built-in logging and monitoring capabilities through tools like Docker logs and Docker stats, which can be used to monitor container health and performance metrics.

Once all traffic has been successfully routed to the green environment and the application is running smoothly, the blue environment can be decommissioned or repurposed for future deployments. However, it is important to retain the blue environment temporarily to facilitate rollback in case of any issues with the green environment.

In summary, blue-green deployment with Docker enables organizations to deploy software updates with minimal downtime and risk by maintaining two identical production environments and gradually transitioning traffic between them. By leveraging container orchestration platforms like Docker Swarm or Kubernetes and implementing robust traffic routing and monitoring mechanisms, organizations can achieve seamless and reliable deployments of containerized applications.

Implementing Canary Releases for Continuous

Deployment is a crucial strategy for minimizing the risks associated with deploying new software updates or features by gradually rolling out changes to a subset of users before making them available to the entire user base. In a canary release, a small percentage of users, often referred to as "canaries," are exposed to the new version of the application or feature while the majority of users continue to use the stable version. This approach allows organizations to gather feedback, monitor performance, and detect any issues or anomalies before fully deploying the changes.

To implement canary releases effectively, organizations leverage container orchestration platforms like Docker Swarm or Kubernetes, which provide robust deployment and scaling capabilities. These platforms enable organizations to define deployment strategies, manage multiple versions of applications simultaneously, and control traffic routing to direct users to specific versions based on predefined criteria.

The first step in implementing a canary release with Docker is to set up a deployment pipeline that automates the process of building, testing, and deploying new versions of the application. Continuous integration and continuous deployment (CI/CD) tools like Jenkins, GitLab CI/CD, or CircleCI can be used to automate this pipeline, triggering deployments whenever changes are pushed to the source code repository.

Once the deployment pipeline is in place, organizations define deployment configurations that specify how new versions of the application should be deployed and how traffic should be routed between different versions. In Docker Swarm, deployment configurations are defined using Docker Compose files or Docker stack files, which specify the services, containers, and deployment parameters for the application.

For example, to deploy a canary release with Docker Swarm, organizations can define two separate services in a Docker Compose file: one for the stable version of the application and another for the canary version. CLI commands like **docker service create** or **docker stack deploy** are then used to deploy the services to the Docker Swarm cluster.

Once the services are deployed, organizations configure traffic routing mechanisms to direct a small percentage of user requests to the canary version of the application while the majority of requests continue to be served by the stable version. In Docker Swarm, this can be achieved using routing mesh or ingress routing, which allow organizations to define rules for routing traffic based on service labels or other criteria.

For example, organizations can use CLI commands like **docker service update** to update the routing rules for the canary service, specifying the percentage of traffic to be routed to the canary version. Similarly, in Kubernetes, organizations can use ingress resources or service selectors to configure traffic splitting between different versions of the application.

Throughout the canary release process, organizations monitor key performance metrics and gather feedback from canary users to assess the impact of the changes and identify any issues or regressions. Monitoring tools like Prometheus, Grafana, or Datadog can be used to track metrics such as latency, error rates, and resource utilization, providing insights into the performance and stability of the canary release.

If any issues or anomalies are detected during the canary release, organizations can quickly rollback the changes by reverting the traffic routing configurations to redirect all traffic back to the stable version of the application. CLI commands like **docker service update** or **kubectl apply** can be used to update the routing rules accordingly, ensuring minimal disruption to users.

Once the canary release has been successfully validated and no significant issues are detected, organizations can gradually increase the percentage of traffic routed to the canary version until it encompasses the entire user base. This gradual rollout approach allows organizations to maintain control over the deployment process and minimize the impact of any potential issues on the overall user experience.

In summary, implementing canary releases for continuous deployment with Docker enables organizations to safely and efficiently deploy new software updates or features by gradually rolling out changes to a subset of users before fully deploying them. By leveraging container orchestration platforms like Docker Swarm or Kubernetes and defining robust deployment configurations and traffic routing mechanisms, organizations can mitigate risks, gather feedback, and ensure a smooth transition to new versions of their applications.

Chapter 9: Autoscaling and Resource Management in Docker

Autoscaling containers based on resource usage is a critical aspect of maintaining optimal performance and availability in dynamic containerized environments. Autoscaling allows organizations to automatically adjust the number of container instances running in response to changes in resource demand, ensuring that applications can efficiently handle fluctuations in workload without overprovisioning or underutilizing resources.

One of the primary benefits of autoscaling containers is the ability to dynamically allocate resources based on real-time demand, thereby optimizing resource utilization and minimizing costs. By automatically scaling up or down in response to changes in workload, organizations can ensure that applications have sufficient resources to handle peak traffic periods while also reducing costs during periods of low demand.

To implement autoscaling for containers, organizations typically leverage container orchestration platforms like Kubernetes or Docker Swarm, which provide built-in support for autoscaling based on predefined metrics such as CPU utilization, memory usage, or custom metrics specific to the application workload.

In Kubernetes, autoscaling is achieved using Horizontal Pod Autoscaler (HPA) objects, which automatically adjust the number of replica pods in a deployment based on CPU utilization or other metrics. Organizations can define HPA objects using YAML manifests or CLI commands like **kubectl autoscale**, specifying the target CPU utilization threshold and the minimum and maximum number of replica pods.

For example, to create an HPA object that autoscales a deployment based on CPU utilization, organizations can use the following CLI command:

arduinoCopy code

```
kubectl autoscale deployment <deployment-name> --cpu-percent=<target-cpu-utilization> --min=<min-replicas> --max=<max-replicas>
```

This command creates an HPA object for the specified deployment, specifying the target CPU utilization threshold as a percentage and the minimum and maximum number of replica pods to scale between.

Similarly, in Docker Swarm, autoscaling is achieved using service replicas, which can be dynamically adjusted based on resource usage or other criteria. Organizations can define autoscaling policies using CLI commands like **docker service update**, specifying the desired scaling behavior and conditions.

For example, to enable autoscaling for a Docker Swarm service based on CPU utilization, organizations can use the following CLI command:

phpCopy code

```
docker service update --limit-cpu=<target-cpu-utilization> --replicas=<desired-replicas> <service-name>
```

This command updates the service configuration to enable CPU-based autoscaling, specifying the target CPU utilization threshold and the desired number of replica instances.

Once autoscaling is enabled, the container orchestration platform continuously monitors resource utilization metrics and adjusts the number of container instances as needed to maintain the specified target utilization threshold. If resource utilization exceeds the threshold, the platform automatically scales up by adding more container instances. Conversely, if resource utilization falls below the threshold, the platform scales down by removing container instances to prevent overprovisioning.

By automating the scaling process based on resource usage metrics, autoscaling containers enable organizations to achieve efficient resource utilization, improved application performance, and enhanced scalability and resilience in dynamic containerized environments. With autoscaling, organizations can ensure that their containerized applications remain responsive and available under varying workload conditions, without the need for manual intervention or pre-provisioning of resources.

Efficient resource management is crucial for maximizing the performance and cost-effectiveness of Docker environments. With Docker, organizations can achieve optimal resource utilization by implementing various strategies and best practices tailored to their specific requirements and workload characteristics.

One key strategy for efficient resource management in Docker is to accurately allocate resources to containerized applications based on their individual requirements. This involves carefully determining the CPU, memory, and other resource limits for each container to prevent resource contention and ensure fair allocation. Docker provides mechanisms for specifying resource limits at the container level using flags such as **--cpu**, **--memory**, and **--cpus** when running containers with the **docker run** command. For example, organizations can use the following command to run a container with specified CPU and memory limits:

phpCopy code

```
docker run --cpus=<number-of-cpus> --memory=<memory-limit> <image-name>
```

By setting appropriate resource limits, organizations can prevent individual containers from monopolizing resources and ensure that multiple containers can coexist on the same host without performance degradation.

Another important aspect of resource management in Docker is to monitor and analyze resource usage to identify potential bottlenecks and optimize resource allocation. Docker provides built-in support for monitoring resource usage at the container, service, and host levels using commands like **docker stats**, **docker service ps**, and **docker node inspect**. These commands allow organizations to view real-time metrics such as CPU and memory usage for individual containers, services, and nodes, enabling them to identify resource-intensive applications or services and take appropriate actions to optimize resource allocation.

In addition to monitoring resource usage, organizations can also implement automated scaling mechanisms to dynamically adjust resource allocation based on workload demand. Docker Swarm and Kubernetes, two popular container orchestration platforms, provide built-in support for autoscaling based on predefined metrics such as CPU and memory utilization. Organizations can define autoscaling policies using YAML manifests or CLI commands, specifying the target utilization thresholds and the minimum and maximum number of replica pods or service instances. For example, in Kubernetes, organizations can create Horizontal Pod Autoscaler (HPA) objects to automatically adjust the number of pod replicas based on CPU or memory utilization, while in Docker Swarm, they can use the **docker service update** command to enable autoscaling for services based on CPU or memory usage.

Furthermore, organizations can optimize resource allocation by leveraging container scheduling and placement strategies to distribute containers across multiple hosts or nodes based on resource availability and workload characteristics. Docker Swarm and Kubernetes use sophisticated scheduling algorithms to distribute containers evenly and efficiently across the cluster, considering factors such as resource constraints, affinity, anti-affinity, and node labels. By strategically placing containers on nodes with available resources and balancing the workload across the cluster, organizations can improve resource utilization and maximize performance.

Additionally, organizations can optimize resource management in Docker by implementing container resource sharing and isolation mechanisms to ensure that containers share resources efficiently while maintaining isolation and security. Docker provides features such as container resource limits, cgroups, namespaces, and container networking and storage isolation to prevent resource contention and ensure that containers operate independently without interference from other containers. By carefully configuring resource limits, isolation, and sharing settings, organizations can achieve optimal resource utilization while ensuring that containers remain isolated and secure.

In summary, efficient resource management is essential for maximizing the performance, scalability, and cost-effectiveness of Docker environments. By accurately allocating resources, monitoring resource usage, implementing automated scaling mechanisms, optimizing container scheduling and placement, and ensuring resource sharing and isolation, organizations can achieve efficient resource utilization and maintain high levels of performance and availability in Docker environments.

Chapter 10: High Availability and Disaster Recovery Strategies

High availability (HA) architectures with Docker involve designing resilient systems that minimize downtime and ensure continuous availability of applications and services. Docker provides several features and best practices to design HA architectures that can withstand failures and scale horizontally to meet increasing demand.

At the core of designing HA architectures with Docker is the use of container orchestration platforms like Docker Swarm or Kubernetes. These platforms enable organizations to manage clusters of Docker hosts and automate the deployment, scaling, and management of containerized applications. With Docker Swarm, organizations can create highly available clusters of Docker hosts by running multiple manager nodes and distributing workload across them. Kubernetes, on the other hand, provides advanced features for orchestrating containers at scale, including automatic scaling, rolling updates, and service discovery.

To design an HA architecture with Docker Swarm, organizations typically start by setting up a cluster of Docker hosts using the **docker swarm init** and **docker swarm join** commands to create manager and worker nodes, respectively. Once the cluster is established, organizations can deploy highly available services using Docker services, which automatically distribute containers across multiple nodes and ensure redundancy. By configuring the desired number of replicas for each service and enabling container rescheduling upon failure, organizations can achieve high availability for their applications.

In Kubernetes, HA architectures are built around the concept of pods, which are groups of one or more containers that share the same network namespace and storage volumes. Organizations can deploy HA applications in Kubernetes by creating replica sets or deploying stateful sets to ensure that multiple instances of a pod are running simultaneously across different nodes. Kubernetes automatically monitors the health of pods and restarts or reschedules them in case of failure, ensuring continuous availability of services.

Another important aspect of designing HA architectures with Docker is data persistence and redundancy. Docker provides features like volume plugins and distributed storage drivers to ensure that data is replicated and available even in the event of node failures. Organizations can use Docker volumes to persist data outside of containers and replicate volumes across multiple nodes using plugins like Docker Volume NetApp or Docker Volume Rex-Ray. Similarly, Kubernetes offers persistent volume claims (PVCs) and storage classes to provision persistent storage for stateful applications and ensure data redundancy and availability.

In addition to container orchestration and data persistence, load balancing is critical for achieving high availability in Docker architectures. Docker Swarm and

Kubernetes both support built-in load balancing mechanisms that distribute incoming traffic across multiple instances of a service or pod. Organizations can configure load balancers like Docker's built-in ingress network or Kubernetes' ingress controllers to route traffic to healthy instances and automatically adjust load balancing configurations based on application demand.

Furthermore, designing HA architectures with Docker involves implementing monitoring and alerting systems to detect and respond to failures proactively. Docker provides built-in monitoring tools like Docker Healthcheck and Docker Stats to monitor the health and performance of containers and services. Organizations can use these tools to set up alerts and notifications for critical events, such as container crashes or resource exhaustion, and take remedial actions automatically using orchestration platforms like Docker Swarm or Kubernetes.

In summary, designing high availability architectures with Docker requires careful planning and implementation of various features and best practices, including container orchestration, data persistence, load balancing, and monitoring. By leveraging Docker Swarm or Kubernetes and following best practices for containerized applications, organizations can build resilient architectures that ensure continuous availability and fault tolerance for their mission-critical services.

Disaster recovery planning for Dockerized environments

is a critical aspect of ensuring business continuity and minimizing the impact of unexpected events such as system failures, natural disasters, or cyberattacks. Docker offers several tools and best practices to help organizations implement robust disaster recovery strategies and restore operations quickly in the event of a disaster.

One fundamental aspect of disaster recovery planning is creating regular backups of Docker containers, images, volumes, and configuration files. Docker provides built-in commands and tools to facilitate backup and restoration tasks. For example, organizations can use the **docker export** command to export container filesystems as tar archives, which can then be stored securely in a backup repository or cloud storage service. Similarly, the **docker commit** command can be used to create snapshots of running containers as images, allowing for easy restoration in case of container failure or data corruption.

Moreover, Docker volumes play a crucial role in disaster recovery by storing persistent data outside of containers and enabling data replication and backup. Organizations can use volume plugins like Docker Volume NetApp or Docker Volume Rex-Ray to replicate volumes across multiple nodes or cloud regions, ensuring data redundancy and availability in the event of a disaster. Additionally, Docker Swarm and Kubernetes offer features for scheduling containers with specific volume requirements and automatically migrating volumes between nodes to maintain data integrity during failover events.

Another key aspect of disaster recovery planning is testing and validating recovery procedures to ensure they work as expected when needed. Organizations should regularly conduct disaster recovery drills and tabletop exercises to simulate different failure scenarios and validate the effectiveness of their recovery plans. By practicing disaster recovery procedures in a controlled environment, organizations can identify potential issues or gaps in their plans and make necessary adjustments to improve resilience and readiness.

Furthermore, organizations should consider leveraging Docker's support for multi-cloud and hybrid cloud deployments to enhance disaster recovery capabilities. By deploying Dockerized applications across multiple cloud providers or data centers, organizations can minimize the risk of data loss or service disruption caused by a single point of failure. Docker Swarm and Kubernetes offer features for deploying applications across distributed environments and automatically failover and migrate workloads between clusters to maintain availability and performance.

In addition to technical measures, disaster recovery planning for Dockerized environments should also include comprehensive documentation and communication strategies to ensure all stakeholders are aware of their roles and responsibilities during a disaster. Organizations should document recovery procedures, contact information for key personnel, and escalation paths for resolving issues effectively. Regular communication and coordination among teams are essential for executing recovery plans efficiently and minimizing downtime during a disaster.

Furthermore, organizations should consider implementing proactive monitoring and alerting systems to detect potential issues or anomalies in Dockerized environments and take preemptive actions to mitigate risks. Docker provides built-in monitoring tools like Docker Healthcheck and Docker Stats, which can be integrated with third-party monitoring solutions to provide real-time visibility into the health and performance of containers and services. By monitoring key metrics such as container uptime, resource utilization, and network traffic, organizations can identify potential issues early and take proactive measures to prevent service disruptions or data loss.

In summary, disaster recovery planning for Dockerized environments requires a combination of technical measures, testing and validation procedures, documentation and communication strategies, and proactive monitoring and alerting systems. By implementing robust disaster recovery strategies and best practices, organizations can minimize the impact of unexpected events and ensure continuous availability and resilience for their Dockerized applications and services.

BOOK 4

EXPERT DOCKER
BUILDING COMPLEX MICROSERVICES ARCHITECTURES

ROB BOTWRIGHT

Chapter 1: Introduction to Microservices Architecture

Understanding microservices principles is crucial for designing and implementing scalable, resilient, and maintainable software architectures. Microservices architecture is a software development approach where applications are composed of small, independent services that are organized around specific business capabilities. These services are built, deployed, and managed independently, allowing teams to work on different parts of the application simultaneously and deploy updates without affecting the entire system.

One of the key principles of microservices is service autonomy. Each microservice is a self-contained unit with its own database, business logic, and user interface (if applicable). This autonomy allows teams to develop and deploy services independently, enabling faster iteration and innovation. To implement service autonomy, developers use containerization technologies like Docker to encapsulate each microservice and its dependencies into lightweight, portable containers.

Another important principle of microservices is loose coupling. Microservices communicate with each other through well-defined APIs, typically using lightweight protocols such as HTTP or messaging queues. This loose coupling enables teams to replace or upgrade individual services without impacting other parts of the system, promoting flexibility and agility. To achieve loose coupling, developers use tools like Docker Compose or Kubernetes to manage service discovery, load balancing, and communication between microservices.

Additionally, microservices adhere to the single responsibility principle, which states that each service should have a single responsibility and perform it well. This principle helps keep services small, focused, and easy to understand, which in turn improves maintainability and reduces complexity. Developers can use domain-driven design (DDD) techniques to identify and define the boundaries of microservices based on business capabilities and domain concepts.

Scalability is another fundamental principle of microservices architecture. Microservices are designed to be horizontally scalable, meaning that instances of a service can be added or removed dynamically to handle changes in load or demand. Developers use container orchestration platforms like Kubernetes to automatically scale services based on predefined metrics such as CPU utilization or request latency. With Kubernetes, scaling a service is as simple as running the **kubectl scale** command with the desired number of replicas.

Resilience is also a key principle of microservices architecture. Since microservices run independently, failures in one service should not cascade to other parts of the system. To achieve resilience, developers implement fault-tolerant strategies such as retries, circuit breakers, and fallback mechanisms in their microservices. Tools like Istio or Envoy can help developers manage service-to-service communication and apply resilience patterns such as circuit breaking and rate limiting.

Furthermore, microservices promote continuous delivery and deployment practices, enabling teams to deliver new features and updates to production quickly and safely. Continuous integration (CI) pipelines automatically build, test, and deploy microservices whenever changes are made to the codebase. Developers use CI/CD tools like Jenkins or GitLab CI to automate the deployment process and ensure consistency and reliability across environments.

Lastly, monitoring and observability are essential principles of microservices architecture. With microservices, it's important to have visibility into the health and performance of individual services and the overall system. Developers use monitoring tools like Prometheus or Grafana to collect and visualize metrics such as request latency, error rates, and resource utilization. Additionally, distributed tracing tools like Jaeger or Zipkin help developers trace requests as they flow through multiple microservices, making it easier to diagnose and debug issues in complex distributed systems.

In summary, understanding microservices principles is essential for building modern, scalable, and resilient software architectures. By adhering to principles such as service autonomy, loose coupling, single responsibility, scalability, resilience, continuous delivery, and monitoring, developers can design and implement microservices-based applications that are flexible, maintainable, and able to meet the evolving needs of the business.

Microservices architecture offers a plethora of advantages over traditional monolithic architectures, making it a popular choice for building modern, scalable, and resilient software systems. One of the primary advantages of microservices architecture is its ability to enable faster development and deployment cycles. With microservices, teams can work on individual services independently, allowing for parallel development and deployment. This results in faster time-to-market for new features and updates. To leverage this advantage, teams often use version control systems like Git to manage the codebase for each microservice. The **git clone** command is used to create a local copy of the repository, while **git checkout** allows developers to switch between branches to work on different features or fixes simultaneously.
Another key advantage of microservices architecture is scalability. Microservices are designed to be independently scalable, meaning that teams can scale

individual services based on demand without affecting other parts of the system. This enables organizations to handle sudden spikes in traffic or load more effectively. Container orchestration platforms like Kubernetes or Docker Swarm are commonly used to automate the scaling process. With Kubernetes, for example, teams can use the **kubectl scale** command to scale the number of replicas for a specific deployment based on predefined metrics such as CPU utilization or request latency.

Furthermore, microservices architecture promotes resilience and fault tolerance. Since services are decoupled and run independently, failures in one service are less likely to impact other parts of the system. This makes it easier to isolate and recover from failures, improving overall system reliability. To enhance resilience, teams implement strategies such as retries, circuit breakers, and fallback mechanisms in their microservices. For example, the **kubectl exec** command can be used to manually trigger a retry of a failed operation within a container, while tools like Istio or Envoy help implement circuit breaking and rate limiting.

Additionally, microservices architecture enhances flexibility and agility. With microservices, teams have the freedom to choose the most appropriate technology stack for each service based on its specific requirements. This flexibility enables teams to adopt new technologies and frameworks more easily, leading to innovation and faster adaptation to changing business needs. For instance, developers can use different programming languages, databases, and frameworks for different microservices based on factors such as performance, scalability, and developer expertise. To manage the diverse technology stack, teams often use containerization technologies like Docker to package and deploy microservices consistently across different environments.

Moreover, microservices architecture improves maintainability and modularity. By breaking down applications into smaller, more manageable components, teams can better understand, update, and refactor codebases. This makes it easier to maintain and evolve software systems over time, reducing the risk of technical debt and code complexity. To ensure code quality and consistency across microservices, teams use practices such as code reviews, automated testing, and continuous integration (CI). Tools like Jenkins or GitLab CI automate the testing and deployment process, ensuring that changes are thoroughly tested before being deployed to production.

Furthermore, microservices architecture facilitates easier integration with third-party services and APIs. Since microservices communicate through well-defined APIs, it's easier to integrate with external systems and services. This enables organizations to leverage existing services and APIs to enhance their applications without reinventing the wheel. To

integrate with external services, developers often use tools like REST clients or SDKs provided by service providers. For example, the **curl** command can be used to make HTTP requests to external APIs, while SDKs provide higher-level abstractions and functionality for interacting with specific services.
In summary, microservices architecture offers numerous advantages, including faster development and deployment cycles, scalability, resilience, flexibility, maintainability, and easier integration with third-party services. By embracing microservices principles and leveraging appropriate tools and technologies, organizations can build modern, scalable, and resilient software systems that meet the evolving needs of their users and business.

Chapter 2: Design Patterns for Microservices with Docker

Architectural patterns play a crucial role in designing and implementing microservices-based systems, providing guidance on how to structure and organize individual services to achieve desired qualities such as scalability, resilience, and maintainability. One commonly used architectural pattern in microservices is the **API Gateway** pattern. In this pattern, an API gateway acts as a single entry point for clients to interact with the system. It handles incoming requests, routes them to the appropriate microservices, and aggregates the responses before sending them back to the client. The API gateway also handles cross-cutting concerns such as authentication, authorization, and rate limiting. To implement an API gateway, developers can use tools like NGINX or Envoy, configuring routing rules and middleware as needed.

Another important architectural pattern for microservices is the **Service Mesh** pattern. In a microservices architecture, communication between services is critical, and the service mesh pattern provides a way to manage this communication in a scalable and resilient manner. A service mesh consists of a dedicated infrastructure layer responsible for handling service-to-service communication, including load balancing, service discovery, encryption, and observability. Tools like Istio and Linkerd are commonly used to implement service meshes in Kubernetes environments. With Istio, for example, developers can use the **istioctl** command to configure routing rules, traffic policies, and telemetry collection for microservices.

Furthermore, the **Event-Driven Architecture (EDA)** pattern is widely used in microservices systems to enable asynchronous communication and loose coupling between services. In this pattern, services communicate with each other by producing and consuming events, which are typically published to a message broker or event bus. This decouples the producers and consumers of events, allowing services to evolve independently. Apache Kafka and RabbitMQ are popular choices for implementing event-driven architectures. Developers can use the Kafka command-line tools to create topics, produce and consume messages, and configure consumer groups. For example, the **kafka-topics.sh** command can be used to create a new topic, while the **kafka-console-consumer.sh** command can be used to consume messages from a topic.

Additionally, the **Saga Pattern** is used to manage distributed transactions across multiple microservices in a consistent and reliable manner. In a microservices architecture, traditional ACID transactions are often challenging to implement due to the distributed nature of the system. Sagas provide an alternative approach by breaking down long-running transactions into a series of smaller, independent steps or compensating actions. Each step in the saga is executed by a separate microservice, and if a step fails, compensating actions are triggered to rollback or undo the changes made by previous steps. Tools like Axon Framework and Eventuate are specifically designed to support saga-based transaction management in microservices architectures.

Moreover, the **CQRS (Command Query Responsibility Segregation)** pattern is commonly used in microservices systems to separate read and write operations for improved scalability and performance. In CQRS, commands represent actions that modify the state of the system, while queries retrieve data without modifying state. By separating the responsibilities for handling commands and queries, developers can optimize each part of the system independently. Event sourcing is often used in conjunction with CQRS to store and replay domain events for building materialized views. Tools like Axon Framework and Lagom provide abstractions and utilities for implementing CQRS and event sourcing in microservices-based systems.

Furthermore, the **Hexagonal Architecture** pattern, also known as Ports and Adapters, is valuable for designing microservices that are highly decoupled and testable. In this pattern, the core business logic of the microservice is encapsulated within the hexagon, while external dependencies such as databases, message brokers, and external services are treated as adapters. This allows developers to easily swap out or mock external dependencies for testing purposes, making the microservice more resilient to changes and easier to maintain. To implement the Hexagonal Architecture pattern, developers can use frameworks like Spring Boot or Micronaut, defining interfaces for external dependencies and providing different implementations as needed.

In summary, architectural patterns play a crucial role in designing and implementing microservices-based systems, providing guidance on how to structure and organize individual services to achieve desired qualities such as scalability, resilience, and maintainability. By understanding and applying these patterns effectively, developers can build robust, flexible, and scalable microservices architectures that meet the evolving needs of their applications and users. Implementing microservices design patterns with Docker is essential for building scalable, resilient, and maintainable microservices architectures. Docker provides a lightweight and portable containerization platform that enables developers to package each microservice along with its dependencies into a container, ensuring consistency across different environments. One of the key microservices design patterns that can be implemented with Docker is the Service Discovery and Registration pattern. In this pattern, each microservice instance registers itself with a service registry upon startup, allowing other services to discover and communicate with it dynamically. Docker provides built-in support for service discovery and registration through Docker Swarm mode or Kubernetes. In Docker Swarm mode, developers can use the docker service create command to create a service and specify a unique service name. For example, to create a service named "my-service" with three replicas, the following command can be used: docker service create --name my-service --replicas 3 my-image. This command creates a service named "my-service" using the specified Docker image and scales it to three replicas. Similarly, in Kubernetes, developers can define a Kubernetes Service object to expose a set of pods as a network service, and Kubernetes takes care of service discovery and load balancing. Developers can use the kubectl create command to create a Kubernetes Service object from a YAML file. For example, the following YAML definition creates a Kubernetes Service named "my-service" that exposes port 80:```yaml apiVersion: v1 kind: Service metadata: name: my-service spec: selector: app: my-app ports: - protocol: TCP port: 80 targetPort: 8080

Chapter 3: Service Discovery and Load Balancing

Service discovery mechanisms play a crucial role in the architecture of microservices, facilitating the dynamic location and communication between services in a distributed environment. Without efficient service discovery, microservices would struggle to communicate with each other as they scale and change. There are several service discovery mechanisms used in microservices architectures, each with its own advantages and implementation strategies.

One of the widely adopted service discovery mechanisms is the **Client-Side Discovery** pattern. In this pattern, the responsibility of service discovery lies with the client application. When a client needs to communicate with a service, it queries a service registry or discovery server to obtain the network location of the desired service instance. This approach provides flexibility and decouples the client from specific service instances, allowing for dynamic service resolution based on runtime conditions. To implement client-side discovery with Docker-based microservices, developers can use tools like Consul, Eureka, or ZooKeeper as service registries. For instance, Consul provides a simple HTTP API and DNS interface for service registration and discovery. Developers can use the Consul CLI tool to register services and query the registry for service locations. To register a service with Consul, the following command can be used: **consul services register my-service.json**. This command registers a service named "my-service" using the configuration specified in the JSON file.

Another common service discovery mechanism is **Server-Side Discovery**, also known as **Service Registry** pattern. In this pattern, a centralized service registry or discovery server maintains a registry of all available service instances along with their network locations. When a client needs to communicate with a service, it queries the service registry to obtain the network location of the desired service instance. Unlike client-side discovery, where the client is responsible for service resolution, server-side discovery centralizes the discovery logic in the registry server, simplifying client implementations. Docker-based microservices can leverage tools like Netflix Eureka or HashiCorp Consul as service registries. For example, developers can deploy Eureka server instances as Docker containers and configure microservices to register themselves with the Eureka server. To deploy an Eureka server using Docker, developers can use the following command: **docker run -d -p 8761:8761 netflixoss/eureka**.

A third service discovery mechanism is **DNS-Based Service Discovery**, where service instances are assigned unique DNS names that clients can use to locate them. When a service instance starts up, it registers its DNS name with a DNS server, which resolves DNS queries from clients to the appropriate service instances. DNS-based service discovery provides a lightweight and decentralized approach to service discovery, leveraging existing DNS infrastructure for resolution. In Docker-based microservices, developers can configure DNS-based service discovery using tools like CoreDNS or dnsmasq. For instance, developers can deploy CoreDNS as a Docker container and configure it to resolve service names to IP addresses dynamically.

Furthermore, container orchestration platforms like Docker Swarm and Kubernetes offer built-in service discovery capabilities. In Docker Swarm, services are automatically registered with an internal DNS service, allowing other services within the Swarm to discover and communicate with them using their service names. Similarly, Kubernetes provides a built-in DNS service that resolves service names to IP addresses within the Kubernetes cluster. Developers can leverage these native service discovery mechanisms when deploying microservices on Docker Swarm or Kubernetes clusters.

In summary, service discovery mechanisms are essential components of microservices architectures, enabling dynamic communication between services in distributed environments. Whether using client-side discovery, server-side discovery, DNS-based discovery, or native platform mechanisms provided by Docker Swarm or Kubernetes, choosing the right service discovery approach depends on factors such as scalability, resilience, and operational requirements of the microservices application. By understanding and implementing effective service discovery mechanisms, developers can build robust and scalable microservices architectures that meet the demands of modern cloud-native applications.

Load balancing strategies are crucial components in the design and deployment of microservices architectures, ensuring optimal distribution of incoming traffic across multiple service instances to improve performance, reliability, and scalability. There are various load balancing techniques and tools available for microservices environments, each tailored to specific use cases and requirements.

One of the most common load balancing strategies used in microservices architectures is **Round Robin Load Balancing**. In this approach, incoming requests are distributed across a pool of service instances in a cyclic manner, ensuring that each instance receives an equal share of the traffic. Round Robin Load Balancing is simple to implement and does not require complex configuration, making it suitable for scenarios where service instances have similar processing capabilities and resource utilization. To configure Round Robin Load Balancing for microservices deployed on Docker Swarm, developers can define a service with multiple replicas, and Swarm's built-in load balancer will distribute incoming requests evenly among the replicas. For example, the following command creates a service named "my-service" with three replicas: **docker service create --replicas 3 my-service**.

Another widely used load balancing strategy is **Least Connections Load Balancing**. In this approach, incoming requests are forwarded to the service instance with the fewest active connections, aiming to evenly distribute the load and prevent overloading of individual instances. Least Connections Load Balancing is particularly effective in scenarios where service instances have varying processing capacities or experience fluctuating traffic patterns. To implement Least Connections Load Balancing in microservices environments, developers can use dedicated load balancing tools such as HAProxy or NGINX. These tools can be deployed as Docker containers and configured to monitor the number of active connections to each service instance, dynamically adjusting traffic distribution based on real-time metrics.

Weighted Round Robin Load Balancing is another variation of the Round Robin approach, where each service instance is assigned a weight value indicating its processing capacity or resource availability. Incoming requests are then distributed based on these weight values, with instances assigned higher weights receiving a larger share of the traffic. Weighted Round Robin Load Balancing allows for fine-grained control over traffic distribution, enabling developers to prioritize certain instances over others based on performance or resource requirements. To implement Weighted Round Robin Load Balancing with Docker Swarm, developers can specify replica counts and placement constraints for each service instance using the **--replicas** and **--constraint** flags. For example, the following command creates two replicas of a service named "my-service" with different weights: **docker service create --replicas 1 --constraint 'node.labels.zone == east' my-service**.

In addition to traditional load balancing techniques, microservices architectures often leverage **Dynamic Load Balancers** capable of adapting to changing traffic conditions and service availability. Dynamic Load Balancers use real-time metrics and health checks to intelligently route traffic to healthy service instances and avoid those experiencing issues or downtime. Tools like Kubernetes Ingress Controllers and service meshes such as Istio and Linkerd provide advanced load balancing capabilities for microservices environments, including traffic routing, load shedding, and circuit breaking. Developers can deploy these tools alongside their microservices applications and configure them to handle load balancing and traffic management tasks automatically.

Furthermore, **Session Affinity** or **Sticky Sessions** can be employed in load balancing strategies to ensure that client requests are consistently routed to the same service instance for the duration of a session. This is particularly useful for stateful applications or scenarios where maintaining session state is necessary. Docker Swarm and Kubernetes support session affinity through features like session stickiness and client IP hashing, allowing developers to ensure consistent session handling across distributed microservices deployments.

In summary, load balancing strategies are essential for optimizing the performance, scalability, and reliability of microservices architectures. Whether using Round Robin, Least Connections, Weighted Round Robin, or dynamic load balancing techniques, choosing the right approach depends on factors such as traffic patterns, resource utilization, and application requirements. By understanding and implementing effective load balancing strategies, developers can ensure that their microservices applications remain responsive and resilient under varying workload conditions.

Chapter 4: Data Management in Microservices

Microservices data patterns play a critical role in shaping the architecture and behavior of distributed systems, particularly concerning how data is managed, stored, and accessed across service boundaries. Among the most debated patterns are "Database Per Service" and "Shared Database." These patterns influence factors such as data isolation, scalability, consistency, and operational complexity, and their selection depends on various considerations such as application requirements, team expertise, and organizational constraints.

The **Database Per Service** pattern advocates for each microservice to have its dedicated database, encapsulating the data it requires to function independently. This approach promotes loose coupling between services and enables teams to make independent decisions regarding data models, schema changes, and database technologies. By isolating data within service boundaries, the Database Per Service pattern enhances the autonomy and agility of individual teams, allowing them to iterate and deploy changes to their respective databases without impacting other services. To implement this pattern, developers typically provision separate database instances or schemas for each microservice using tools like Docker and Kubernetes. For example, the following command creates a MySQL container named "my-service-db" with a custom database schema:

bashCopy code

```
docker run --name my-service-db -e MYSQL_ROOT_PASSWORD=password -e MYSQL_DATABASE=my_database -d mysql:latest
```

While the Database Per Service pattern offers benefits in terms of autonomy and encapsulation, it also introduces challenges related to data consistency, transaction management, and cross-service communication. Achieving data consistency across multiple databases can be complex, especially in scenarios involving distributed transactions or eventual consistency requirements. Additionally, maintaining referential integrity and enforcing data relationships across service boundaries may require implementing compensating transactions or event-driven synchronization mechanisms.

In contrast, the **Shared Database** pattern advocates for multiple microservices to share a common database instance or schema, consolidating data across service boundaries. This approach simplifies data management by centralizing access to a single source of truth and promoting strong consistency guarantees across services. Shared databases facilitate data sharing and communication between services, enabling complex queries, joins, and transactions that span multiple domains. To implement this pattern, developers typically deploy a single database instance accessible to all microservices, configuring access controls and data isolation mechanisms to enforce service boundaries. For example, the following command creates a PostgreSQL container named "shared-db" accessible by multiple microservices:

bashCopy code

```
docker run --name shared-db -e POSTGRES_PASSWORD=password -e POSTGRES_DB=my_database -d postgres:latest
```

While the Shared Database pattern simplifies data management and promotes consistency, it also introduces dependencies and tight coupling between services, making it challenging to evolve and scale independently. Changes to the shared schema or data model may require coordination between multiple teams, potentially leading to deployment bottlenecks and conflicts. Additionally, shared databases pose risks related to data access control, security, and compliance, as any service with access to the database can potentially read or modify sensitive information.

In practice, the choice between Database Per Service and Shared Database patterns depends on various factors such as application complexity, team dynamics, performance requirements, and regulatory constraints. Hybrid approaches, such as using separate databases for transactional and analytical workloads or employing database sharding techniques for scalability, can also be adopted to strike a balance between autonomy and consistency. Ultimately, selecting the right data pattern requires careful consideration of trade-offs and alignment with the broader architectural goals and business objectives.

Data consistency and transactions are fundamental aspects of microservices architecture, influencing the reliability, integrity, and performance of distributed systems. In the context of microservices, achieving data consistency becomes more challenging due to the decentralized nature of service communication and the potential for data duplication and inconsistency across service boundaries. Several strategies and techniques exist to address these challenges and ensure robust data consistency and transaction management in microservices environments.

One common approach to maintaining data consistency in microservices is through **Synchronous Communication**. In synchronous communication, services interact directly with each other via request-response mechanisms, such as HTTP or gRPC. This approach simplifies transaction management by allowing services to coordinate actions within a single transaction boundary, ensuring that changes are either committed or rolled back atomically. For example, consider a scenario where a customer places an order, triggering updates to both the order service and the inventory service. Using synchronous communication, the order service can initiate a transaction that updates both databases atomically, ensuring that the order is only confirmed if there is sufficient inventory available.

To illustrate, suppose you have a microservice architecture with Docker containers running the order service and the inventory service. You can deploy these services using Docker Compose with the following YAML configuration:

yamlCopy code

version: '3' services: order-service: image: order-service:latest ports: - "8080:8080" inventory-service: image: inventory-service:latest ports: - "8081:8081"

This configuration defines two services, each running in its container, and exposes their respective ports for communication.

While synchronous communication simplifies transaction management, it can also introduce challenges related to performance, scalability, and fault tolerance. Synchronous calls are blocking by nature, meaning that services must wait for responses before proceeding, which can lead to increased latency and reduced throughput, especially in high-volume environments. Additionally, synchronous communication can create tight coupling between services, making it harder to evolve and scale independently.

To mitigate the limitations of synchronous communication, **Asynchronous Communication** patterns can be employed. In asynchronous communication, services communicate indirectly through message brokers or event streaming platforms, such as Apache Kafka or RabbitMQ. This decouples producers from consumers, allowing services to exchange messages asynchronously without blocking each other. Asynchronous communication enables eventual consistency, where updates are propagated asynchronously and may take time to reach all replicas or databases. While this approach reduces coupling and improves scalability and fault tolerance, it introduces complexity in managing message ordering, idempotency, and error handling.

To implement asynchronous communication with Docker, you can deploy message brokers or event streaming platforms as separate Docker containers alongside microservices. For instance, deploying Apache Kafka with Docker Compose can be achieved with the following configuration:

yamlCopy code

```
version: '3' services: zookeeper: image:
wurstmeister/zookeeper ports: - "2181:2181"
kafka: image: wurstmeister/kafka ports: -
"9092:9092" environment:
KAFKA_ADVERTISED_LISTENERS:
PLAINTEXT://localhost:9092
KAFKA_LISTENER_SECURITY_PROTOCOL_MAP:
```

```
PLAINTEXT:PLAINTEXT
KAFKA_INTER_BROKER_LISTENER_NAME: PLAINTEXT
KAFKA_ZOOKEEPER_CONNECT: zookeeper:2181
depends_on: - zookeeper
```

This configuration defines Zookeeper and Kafka services, with Kafka depending on Zookeeper for coordination. Kafka exposes port 9092 for communication between producers and consumers.

Another important aspect of ensuring data consistency in microservices is **Event Sourcing**. In event sourcing, services persist changes to their state as a sequence of immutable events, rather than updating a shared database directly. Each event represents a fact or action that occurred within the system, such as "order placed" or "inventory updated." By storing events in a log or append-only datastore, services can reconstruct their state by replaying events sequentially, ensuring that data consistency is maintained even in the presence of failures or concurrent updates. Event sourcing enables auditability, traceability, and resilience, as events can be replayed, analyzed, and reprocessed as needed.

To implement event sourcing with Docker, you can deploy event store databases like Apache Kafka or Apache Pulsar as Docker containers alongside microservices. Additionally, frameworks and libraries such as Axon Framework or Eventuate provide abstractions and tooling to simplify event-driven architecture and event sourcing implementation in Dockerized environments.

Overall, data consistency and transaction management are critical considerations in microservices architecture, requiring careful planning and implementation to ensure reliability, integrity, and performance. By leveraging synchronous and asynchronous communication patterns, along with event sourcing techniques, developers can design resilient and scalable microservices systems that maintain data consistency while supporting distributed transactions and complex workflows.

Chapter 5: Securing Microservices with Docker

Container security is paramount in ensuring the integrity, confidentiality, and availability of applications and data running within containers. As organizations increasingly adopt containerized environments for deploying their applications, it becomes crucial to implement robust security measures to protect against potential vulnerabilities and threats. Container security best practices encompass various aspects, including image security, runtime security, network security, orchestration security, and compliance. By following these best practices, organizations can mitigate risks and maintain a secure containerized environment.

One fundamental aspect of container security is **Image Security**. It involves ensuring that container images are built from trusted sources, free of vulnerabilities, and adhere to security standards. Organizations should use base images from official repositories or trusted sources and regularly update them to incorporate security patches and fixes. Additionally, scanning container images for known vulnerabilities using tools like Trivy, Clair, or Docker Security Scanning is essential. These tools analyze container images for vulnerabilities in their dependencies and provide actionable insights to remediate them. To scan a container image using

Trivy, for example, you can run the following command:

arduinoCopy code

```
trivy image <image_name>
```

This command will scan the specified container image for vulnerabilities and display the results, allowing administrators to take appropriate actions to address any security issues identified.

Runtime security is another critical aspect of container security, focusing on protecting containers during execution. Implementing **Least Privilege** principles, where containers run with minimal permissions and access rights, helps mitigate the risk of unauthorized access and privilege escalation. Utilizing container runtime security tools like SELinux, AppArmor, or seccomp can further restrict container capabilities and enforce security policies. For example, enabling SELinux in Docker can be achieved by configuring the Docker daemon with the **--selinux-enabled** flag or setting the **--security-opt** flag for individual containers.

arduinoCopy code

```
docker run --security-opt label=type:container_runtime_t <image_name>
```

This command instructs Docker to enforce SELinux policies for the specified container, enhancing its runtime security.

Network security is another crucial consideration in containerized environments, given the dynamic and ephemeral nature of container networking. Employing **Network Segmentation** techniques, such as creating separate network namespaces or using network policies in Kubernetes, helps isolate containers and control traffic flow between them. Implementing secure communication protocols like TLS for inter-container communication and encrypting data in transit further enhances network security. Tools like Calico, Cilium, or Istio provide advanced network security features, including network policy enforcement, encryption, and traffic monitoring, in Kubernetes environments.

Copy code

```
kubectl apply -f network-policy.yaml
```

This command applies a network policy defined in a YAML file to enforce communication rules between pods in a Kubernetes cluster, thereby enhancing network security.

Orchestration security is essential for securing container orchestration platforms like Kubernetes or Docker Swarm. Organizations should adhere to security best practices when configuring and managing orchestration platforms, including enabling authentication, authorization, and encryption mechanisms. Implementing Role-Based Access Control (RBAC) to control user access and permissions, enabling audit logging to monitor platform activities, and regularly updating and patching orchestration components are critical steps in ensuring orchestration security. Additionally, scanning Kubernetes manifests and Docker Compose files for security misconfigurations using tools like kubeaudit or Docker Bench for Security helps identify potential vulnerabilities and weaknesses in deployment configurations.

Copy code

```
kubeaudit deployment.yaml
```

This command audits a Kubernetes deployment manifest file for security best practices and potential misconfigurations, allowing administrators to remediate security issues proactively.

Compliance with industry regulations and standards is another vital aspect of container security. Organizations operating in regulated industries must ensure that their containerized environments comply with relevant regulations, such as GDPR, HIPAA, PCI DSS, or ISO 27001. Implementing security controls and practices aligned with these regulations, conducting regular security audits and assessments, and maintaining documentation and logs for compliance purposes are essential for demonstrating adherence to regulatory requirements.

In summary, container security best practices encompass various aspects, including image security, runtime security, network security, orchestration security, and compliance. By following these best practices and leveraging security tools and technologies, organizations can establish a robust security posture for their containerized environments, mitigating risks and ensuring the integrity, confidentiality, and availability of their applications and data.

Securing microservices communications is crucial for protecting sensitive data and ensuring the integrity and confidentiality of interactions between microservices in distributed architectures. Microservices architectures, characterized by their modular and decentralized nature, require robust security mechanisms to prevent unauthorized access, eavesdropping, data tampering, and other security threats. Securing microservices communications involves various techniques and best practices, including encryption, authentication, authorization, and network segmentation.

One fundamental aspect of securing microservices communications is **Transport Layer Security (TLS)** encryption. TLS ensures that data transmitted between microservices is encrypted, preventing unauthorized parties from intercepting and reading sensitive information. Implementing TLS requires generating SSL/TLS certificates for each microservice and configuring them to enable encrypted communication. Tools like OpenSSL or Let's Encrypt can be used to generate SSL/TLS certificates, and web servers like Nginx or Envoy can be configured to terminate TLS connections and forward requests to microservices over encrypted channels.

csharpCopy code

```
openssl req -newkey rsa:2048 -nodes -keyout server.key -x509 -days 365 -out server.crt
```

This command generates a self-signed SSL/TLS certificate and private key pair for securing communication between microservices.

Authentication is another essential aspect of securing microservices communications, ensuring that only authorized entities can access protected resources. Implementing **Mutual TLS (mTLS)** authentication, where both the client and server authenticate each other using SSL/TLS certificates, enhances security by verifying the identity of communicating parties. Each microservice is issued a unique SSL/TLS certificate, and only clients possessing valid certificates signed by a trusted Certificate Authority (CA) can establish connections with microservices. Tools like Istio or Linkerd provide mTLS support and streamline the configuration of mutual authentication between microservices.

Copy code

```
kubectl apply -f istio-mtls.yaml
```

This command enables mutual TLS authentication between microservices in a Kubernetes cluster using Istio, enforcing strict authentication and encryption requirements for communication.

Authorization is another critical aspect of securing microservices communications, controlling access to resources based on the identity and permissions of requesting entities. Implementing **Access Control**

Policies at the microservice level, where permissions are defined and enforced based on user roles or attributes, helps prevent unauthorized access to sensitive data and functionalities. Role-Based Access Control (RBAC) mechanisms can be employed to define granular access policies and assign roles to users or services, ensuring that only authorized entities can perform specific actions within microservices environments. Tools like Open Policy Agent (OPA) or Kubernetes RBAC enable fine-grained access control and policy enforcement in microservices architectures.

Copy code

```
kubectl apply -f rbac-policy.yaml
```

This command applies an RBAC policy defined in a YAML file to enforce access control rules and permissions for microservices within a Kubernetes cluster.

Network segmentation is essential for isolating microservices and controlling communication between them, reducing the attack surface and limiting the impact of potential security breaches. Implementing **Microsegmentation** techniques, where network traffic is segregated into distinct segments or virtual networks based on security policies, helps prevent lateral movement of attackers and restricts communication between microservices to authorized channels. Tools like Calico, AWS VPC, or Azure Virtual Network provide microsegmentation capabilities and enable organizations to define and enforce network policies that govern traffic flow between microservices.

Copy code

```
kubectl apply -f calico-policy.yaml
```

This command applies a network policy defined in a YAML file using Calico, enforcing microsegmentation and restricting communication between microservices based on defined rules.

In summary, securing microservices communications is essential for maintaining the integrity, confidentiality, and availability of data and services in distributed architectures. By implementing encryption, authentication, authorization, and network segmentation techniques, organizations can establish a robust security posture and mitigate the risk of security threats and breaches in microservices environments.

Chapter 6: Event-Driven Architecture with Docker

Event-driven design principles are fundamental concepts in software architecture that emphasize the use of events to trigger and communicate changes within a system. Events represent occurrences or state changes within a system and can include actions, notifications, or updates. Event-driven architecture (EDA) decouples components and enables asynchronous communication between them, facilitating scalability, flexibility, and responsiveness in distributed systems.

One key principle of event-driven design is **Loose Coupling**, which promotes independence and autonomy among system components by minimizing direct dependencies between them. In event-driven architectures, components interact through events, allowing them to operate independently without needing to know the internal details or implementations of other components. This loose coupling enhances system modularity, simplifies maintenance, and enables components to evolve independently, promoting flexibility and scalability.

Another important principle is **Asynchronous Communication**, which enables components to communicate and interact without waiting for immediate responses. In event-driven architectures, components produce and consume events asynchronously, allowing them to continue processing other tasks while waiting for events to occur or be processed. Asynchronous communication reduces latency, improves system responsiveness, and enhances scalability by decoupling the timing of event production and consumption.

Event Sourcing is a principle that involves capturing and storing all changes to the state of a system as a sequence of immutable events. Instead of storing the current state of the system, event sourcing records the series of events that led to the current state, providing a complete audit trail of system behavior over time. Event sourcing enables replaying events to rebuild system state, supporting features like temporal queries, auditing, and debugging. Tools like Apache Kafka or AWS Kinesis facilitate event sourcing by providing scalable and durable event streaming platforms for capturing and processing events.

cssCopy code

```
aws kinesis create-stream --stream-name my-stream
--shard-count 1
```

This command creates an Amazon Kinesis stream named "my-stream" with one shard for capturing and processing events in an event-driven architecture.

Event-Driven Microservices leverage event-driven design principles to build loosely coupled, scalable, and resilient microservices architectures. Each microservice publishes events when state changes occur, and other microservices subscribe to these events to react accordingly. This asynchronous communication pattern enables microservices to operate independently and asynchronously, promoting agility, scalability, and fault tolerance in distributed systems.

Domain-Driven Design (DDD) principles complement event-driven design by emphasizing the modeling of business domains and behaviors using a ubiquitous language shared between technical and domain experts. Events serve as a key part of the ubiquitous language in DDD, representing meaningful business actions or state changes. By aligning event-driven design with DDD principles, developers can create more expressive, domain-centric event schemas that accurately capture and communicate business intent.

Event Choreography and **Event Orchestration** are two approaches to coordinating interactions between microservices in event-driven architectures. Event choreography involves allowing microservices to react to events independently, with no central coordination. In contrast, event orchestration involves using a central orchestrator or workflow engine to coordinate and sequence interactions between microservices based on predefined workflows or business logic. Both approaches have their strengths and weaknesses, and the choice between them depends on factors like complexity, scalability, and maintainability requirements.

In summary, event-driven design principles play a crucial role in building scalable, flexible, and responsive software architectures. By embracing loose coupling, asynchronous communication, event sourcing, and domain-driven design, developers can create resilient, decoupled systems capable of adapting to changing requirements and environments. Event-driven architectures enable organizations to build distributed systems that can efficiently handle complex business logic, support real-time processing, and seamlessly scale to meet growing demands.

Implementing Event-Driven Architecture (EDA) with Docker involves leveraging Docker's containerization technology to build scalable, loosely coupled, and resilient event-driven systems. Docker provides a lightweight and portable runtime environment for deploying and managing microservices, making it well-suited for building event-driven architectures. The key components and techniques for implementing EDA with Docker include containerizing microservices, using message brokers for event communication, deploying event-driven applications with Docker Compose or Kubernetes, and implementing event-driven patterns such as event sourcing, CQRS (Command Query Responsibility Segregation), and event choreography.

Containerizing microservices is a fundamental step in implementing EDA with Docker. Docker containers encapsulate microservices along with their dependencies, libraries, and runtime environments, enabling consistent deployment across different environments. Developers can use Dockerfiles to define the configuration and dependencies of microservices and then build Docker images using the **docker build** command. For example, to build a Docker image for a microservice named "user-service," developers can use the following command:

sqlCopy code

```
docker build -t user-service:v1 .
```

This command builds a Docker image tagged as "user-service:v1" based on the Dockerfile in the current directory.

Once microservices are containerized, they need to communicate with each other asynchronously through events. Message brokers such as Apache Kafka, RabbitMQ, or AWS SQS (Simple Queue Service) are commonly used in event-driven architectures to facilitate event communication between microservices. These message brokers act as centralized event hubs where producers publish events, and consumers subscribe to receive and process those events. Developers can deploy message brokers as Docker containers alongside other microservices using Docker Compose or Kubernetes.

Deploying event-driven applications with Docker Compose simplifies the management of multi-container Docker applications by defining the services, networks, and volumes in a single YAML file. Developers can use Docker Compose to define the configuration of microservices, including their dependencies and communication channels. For example, the following Docker Compose snippet defines a service named "user-service" and its dependency on a Kafka message broker:

yamlCopy code

services: user-service: image: user-service:v1 depends_on: - kafka kafka: image: confluentinc/cp-kafka:latest ports: - "9092:9092"

This configuration specifies two services: "user-service" and "kafka," with "user-service" depending on "kafka" for event communication.

Alternatively, Kubernetes can be used for orchestrating event-driven applications at scale. Kubernetes provides advanced features for managing containerized workloads, including service discovery, load balancing, auto-scaling, and rolling updates. Developers can define Kubernetes manifests (YAML files) to specify the desired state of their application, including deployments, services, ingress rules, and persistent volumes. Kubernetes operators like Strimzi for Kafka or RabbitMQ Operator can be used to deploy and manage message brokers as Kubernetes resources.

In addition to deploying microservices and message brokers, implementing event-driven patterns is essential for building robust and scalable event-driven architectures with Docker. Event sourcing, for example, involves capturing and storing all changes to the state of a system as a sequence of immutable events. Developers can use Docker containers to deploy event sourcing components such as event stores or event processors, ensuring the reliability and durability of event data.

CQRS (Command Query Responsibility Segregation) is another event-driven pattern that separates the responsibilities of handling commands (write operations) and queries (read operations) into distinct components. Docker containers enable developers to deploy command and query services independently, facilitating scalability and flexibility in handling different types of requests.

Event choreography is a decentralized approach to coordinating interactions between microservices in event-driven architectures. Docker containers allow developers to deploy event-driven components autonomously, with each microservice reacting to events and making decisions based on its own logic. This decentralized model reduces dependencies and promotes agility and scalability in distributed systems.

Overall, implementing event-driven architecture with Docker empowers developers to build scalable, resilient, and agile systems that can efficiently handle complex event processing workflows. By containerizing microservices, deploying message brokers, orchestrating applications with Docker Compose or Kubernetes, and embracing event-driven patterns, organizations can leverage the power of Docker to build next-generation event-driven architectures that meet the demands of modern distributed systems.

Chapter 7: Scalability and Performance Optimization Techniques

Horizontal and vertical scaling strategies are essential considerations when designing and deploying microservices architectures to ensure optimal performance, scalability, and resource utilization. Horizontal scaling involves adding more instances of microservices to distribute the workload across multiple nodes, while vertical scaling involves increasing the resources (such as CPU, memory, or storage) allocated to individual instances of microservices.

Horizontal scaling, also known as scaling out, is a common approach to handle increasing traffic and workload demands in microservices architectures. Docker Swarm and Kubernetes are popular container orchestration platforms that support horizontal scaling of microservices. In Docker Swarm, scaling a service horizontally can be achieved using the **docker service scale** command followed by the service name and the desired number of replicas. For example, to scale a service named "user-service" to three replicas, the following command can be used:

sqlCopy code

```
docker service scale user-service=3
```

Similarly, in Kubernetes, horizontal scaling is achieved using the Horizontal Pod Autoscaler (HPA) resource, which automatically adjusts the number of replica pods based on observed CPU utilization or other custom metrics. Developers can define an HPA object in a Kubernetes manifest file to specify the target CPU utilization and minimum/maximum replica counts for a deployment. For instance, the following YAML snippet defines an HPA object for a deployment named "user-deployment" with a target CPU utilization of 50% and a minimum of two replicas:

yamlCopy code

```
apiVersion: autoscaling/v2beta2 kind: HorizontalPodAutoscaler metadata: name: user-deployment-autoscaler spec: scaleTargetRef: apiVersion: apps/v1 kind: Deployment name: user-deployment minReplicas: 2 maxReplicas: 10 metrics: - type: Resource resource: name: cpu targetAverageUtilization: 50
```

Vertical scaling, on the other hand, involves increasing the resources allocated to individual instances of microservices. Docker allows for vertical scaling by specifying resource constraints such as CPU and memory limits for containers using the **docker run** command or Docker Compose YAML files. For example, to run a container with 2 CPU cores and 4GB of memory, the following Docker run command can be used:

arduinoCopy code

```
docker run --cpus=2 --memory=4g my-container-image
```

In Kubernetes, vertical scaling is achieved through the Vertical Pod Autoscaler (VPA) resource, which automatically adjusts the resource requests and limits of pods based on resource usage metrics. Developers can configure VPA objects in Kubernetes to specify target resource utilization thresholds and resource allocation constraints for pods. Here's an example of a VPA object definition for a deployment named "user-deployment" with target CPU utilization of 50%:

yamlCopy code

apiVersion: autoscaling.k8s.io/v1 kind: VerticalPodAutoscaler metadata: name: user-deployment-vpa spec: targetRef: apiVersion: "apps/v1" kind: Deployment name: user-deployment updatePolicy: updateMode: "Auto"

Both horizontal and vertical scaling strategies have their advantages and trade-offs. Horizontal scaling offers better fault tolerance and scalability by distributing the workload across multiple instances, but it may require additional effort to manage service discovery, load balancing, and data consistency. Vertical scaling, on the other hand, provides improved performance and resource utilization for individual instances but may have limitations in terms of scalability and fault tolerance.

In summary, understanding and implementing horizontal and vertical scaling strategies are crucial aspects of designing and deploying microservices architectures. By leveraging container orchestration platforms like Docker Swarm and Kubernetes, developers can efficiently scale microservices to meet the dynamic demands of modern applications while optimizing resource utilization and ensuring high availability and performance.

Performance optimization techniques are crucial for ensuring the efficient operation of Dockerized microservices in modern software development environments. By fine-tuning various aspects of containerized applications, developers can enhance resource utilization, reduce latency, and improve overall system responsiveness. Next, we will explore a variety of performance optimization strategies and best practices tailored specifically for Dockerized microservices.

One fundamental aspect of performance optimization in Dockerized microservices is container resource allocation. Properly configuring resource limits, such as CPU and memory constraints, ensures that containers have sufficient resources to execute their tasks efficiently without overutilizing system resources or causing resource contention. Docker provides command-line options and Docker Compose configuration parameters to set resource limits for containers. For example, the **--cpus** and **--memory** flags in the **docker run** command allow specifying the number of CPU cores and memory allocation for containers, respectively. Similarly, Docker Compose YAML files support the **cpu_limit** and **mem_limit** properties to define resource limits for services.

In addition to resource allocation, optimizing Docker container images can significantly improve performance and reduce container startup time. Utilizing lightweight base images, such as Alpine Linux or BusyBox, and minimizing the number of layers in Docker images can help reduce image size and improve container startup time. Docker provides various commands, such as **docker build** and **docker images**, to manage and inspect Docker images. By leveraging multi-stage builds and efficient caching mechanisms, developers can streamline the Docker image build process and produce leaner, more optimized container images.

Furthermore, optimizing Docker container networking can enhance communication latency and throughput between microservices running in containers. Docker offers several networking modes, including bridge, host, and overlay networks, each with its own performance characteristics and use cases. By selecting the appropriate networking mode and configuring network settings, developers can optimize container networking performance based on the specific requirements of their microservices architecture. For example, deploying containers on the same host using the host network mode can eliminate the overhead of Docker's internal networking stack and improve inter-container communication performance.

Container orchestration platforms like Docker Swarm and Kubernetes provide advanced features for performance optimization, such as horizontal scaling and load balancing. Horizontal scaling allows dynamically adding or removing container instances based on resource utilization metrics, ensuring optimal resource allocation and workload distribution. Kubernetes Horizontal Pod Autoscaler (HPA) and Docker Swarm service scaling commands enable automatic scaling of microservices based on CPU and memory usage metrics. Additionally, load balancing mechanisms, such as Kubernetes Service and Docker Swarm routing mesh, distribute incoming traffic across multiple container instances to prevent overloading individual containers and ensure high availability and fault tolerance.

Another critical aspect of performance optimization in Dockerized microservices is efficient data management and storage. By leveraging Docker volumes and persistent storage solutions, developers can ensure fast and reliable access to data for microservices without sacrificing performance. Docker volumes allow containers to share data with host filesystems or other containers efficiently, while persistent storage solutions, such as Docker volumes or external storage providers like Amazon EBS or Google Cloud Storage, enable data persistence and resilience across container restarts and redeployments.

Furthermore, optimizing application code and containerized services can have a significant impact on overall performance and scalability. Adopting best practices for microservices development, such as asynchronous communication, caching, and parallel processing, can improve application responsiveness and throughput. Additionally, leveraging container orchestration features like service discovery, health checks, and rolling updates can enhance service availability, resilience, and performance in dynamic containerized environments.

In summary, performance optimization is a critical aspect of Dockerized microservices architecture, ensuring efficient resource utilization, low latency, and high throughput. By following best practices for container resource allocation, image optimization, networking configuration, orchestration, data management, and application design, developers can maximize the performance and scalability of their Dockerized microservices applications. Continuous monitoring, benchmarking, and tuning are essential to identify performance bottlenecks and fine-tune system configurations to meet evolving workload demands and performance requirements.

Chapter 8: Containerizing Legacy Applications

Modernizing legacy applications with Docker is a pivotal step in the journey towards digital transformation for many organizations, enabling them to leverage the benefits of containerization, microservices architecture, and cloud-native technologies. Legacy applications, typically monolithic in nature, are often characterized by tightly coupled components, outdated dependencies, and deployment challenges. Docker offers several strategies and best practices for modernizing legacy applications, allowing organizations to enhance scalability, agility, and resilience while minimizing disruption to existing workflows.

One approach to modernizing legacy applications with Docker is the lift-and-shift migration strategy, which involves packaging the entire legacy application into Docker containers without making significant changes to the underlying codebase. This approach enables organizations to quickly migrate legacy applications to containerized environments with minimal code refactoring or rearchitecting. Docker provides tools such as Docker Desktop and Docker CLI for building Docker images from legacy application codebases and running containers locally for testing and validation.

Another strategy for modernizing legacy applications with Docker is the refactor and re-platform approach, which involves breaking down monolithic applications into smaller, more manageable components and refactoring them into microservices. Docker facilitates this process by providing a lightweight, portable runtime environment for individual microservices, enabling developers to decompose monolithic applications into loosely coupled services that can be independently deployed, scaled, and updated. Docker Compose allows developers to define multi-container applications comprising microservices using a simple YAML-based configuration file, making it easier to manage complex application architectures.

Containerizing legacy applications with Docker also offers organizations the opportunity to modernize their infrastructure and adopt cloud-native deployment practices. By running legacy applications in Docker containers, organizations can leverage cloud platforms such as Amazon Web Services (AWS), Microsoft Azure, and Google Cloud Platform (GCP) to deploy and manage containerized workloads at scale. Docker Swarm and Kubernetes are popular container orchestration platforms that provide advanced features for deploying and managing containerized applications in cloud environments, including auto-scaling, load balancing, and service discovery.

Furthermore, Docker enables organizations to implement modern DevOps practices, such as continuous integration (CI) and continuous delivery (CD), to streamline the software development lifecycle and accelerate the delivery of new features and updates. By integrating Docker with CI/CD pipelines, organizations can automate the build, test, and deployment processes for containerized applications, ensuring consistency and reliability across development, testing, and production environments. Docker Hub and Docker Trusted Registry (DTR) are Docker's container image registries that provide version control, image scanning, and security features to support CI/CD workflows.

One of the key benefits of modernizing legacy applications with Docker is improved scalability and resource utilization. Docker's lightweight, isolated containers enable organizations to scale individual components of legacy applications horizontally based on demand, optimizing resource allocation and improving application performance. Docker Swarm and Kubernetes provide built-in features for auto-scaling containerized workloads based on CPU and memory utilization, ensuring optimal resource utilization and efficient handling of fluctuating workloads.

Additionally, Docker facilitates the adoption of modern security practices and compliance standards for legacy applications. Docker's built-in security features, such as container isolation, resource constraints, and image signing, help organizations enforce security policies and protect sensitive data in containerized environments. Docker Content Trust (DCT) and Docker Security Scanning provide tools for verifying the integrity and authenticity of container images, mitigating the risk of security vulnerabilities and supply chain attacks.

In summary, modernizing legacy applications with Docker offers organizations a cost-effective, low-risk approach to accelerating digital transformation and embracing cloud-native technologies. By leveraging Docker's containerization platform and ecosystem of tools and services, organizations can decompose monolithic applications into microservices, adopt modern DevOps practices, and achieve greater scalability, agility, and resilience in their software delivery pipelines. Continuous innovation and collaboration within the Docker community ensure that organizations can stay ahead of evolving technology trends and drive business value through modernized legacy applications.

Containerizing legacy systems presents a myriad of challenges, ranging from compatibility issues to architectural complexities, but with careful planning and the right tools, organizations can overcome these obstacles and unlock the benefits of containerization for their legacy applications. One of the primary challenges in containerizing legacy systems is dealing with outdated dependencies and software versions that may not be compatible with modern container runtimes. In many cases, legacy applications rely on specific versions of operating system libraries, middleware, or runtime environments that are not readily available in containerized environments. To address this challenge, organizations can leverage Docker's multi-stage build feature to create lightweight, portable container images that include only the necessary dependencies and libraries required to run the legacy application. By isolating dependencies within the container image, organizations can ensure consistency and reproducibility across different deployment environments.

Another challenge in containerizing legacy systems is managing stateful components, such as databases or file systems, that require persistent storage and data management capabilities. Unlike stateless microservices, stateful applications pose unique challenges for containerization, as they often rely on external storage volumes or databases that must be carefully managed to ensure data consistency and integrity. Docker provides several solutions for managing stateful components in containerized environments, including Docker volumes and Docker Compose for defining multi-container applications with shared storage volumes. By separating data from the application logic and leveraging container orchestration platforms like Docker Swarm or Kubernetes, organizations can ensure high availability, data redundancy, and disaster recovery for stateful applications running in containers.

Furthermore, organizations face challenges in ensuring security and compliance when containerizing legacy systems, particularly if the legacy application contains sensitive data or proprietary information. Docker provides several built-in security features, such as container isolation, resource constraints, and image signing, to mitigate the risk of security vulnerabilities and unauthorized access to containerized applications. Additionally, organizations can leverage Docker Security Scanning and vulnerability management tools to identify and remediate security issues in container images before they are deployed in production environments. Implementing security best practices, such as least privilege access controls and network segmentation, can further enhance the security posture of containerized legacy systems and protect against potential threats and attacks.

Another significant challenge in containerizing legacy systems is maintaining compatibility with existing infrastructure and workflows, such as build pipelines, deployment processes, and monitoring tools. Docker provides a flexible and extensible platform that integrates seamlessly with existing development and operations workflows, enabling organizations to containerize legacy applications without disrupting existing processes. Docker Hub and Docker Trusted Registry (DTR) provide centralized repositories for storing and managing container images, while Docker Compose and Docker Swarm offer tools for defining and deploying multi-container applications in a consistent and reproducible manner. By adopting a container-first approach to application development and modernizing existing workflows with Docker-compatible tools and technologies, organizations can streamline the containerization process and accelerate the adoption of containerized legacy systems.

Additionally, organizations may encounter challenges related to performance optimization and resource utilization when containerizing legacy systems, particularly if the legacy application is resource-intensive or requires specialized hardware or software configurations. Docker provides several features for optimizing container performance, such as resource limits, CPU and memory constraints, and container health checks, to ensure optimal resource utilization and application stability. Additionally, organizations can leverage Docker Swarm or Kubernetes to distribute containerized workloads across multiple nodes and scale applications dynamically based on demand. By monitoring container performance metrics and optimizing resource allocation, organizations can maximize the efficiency and scalability of containerized legacy systems and deliver a seamless user experience to end-users.

In summary, containerizing legacy systems presents unique challenges related to compatibility, state management, security, and performance optimization, but with the right strategies and tools, organizations can overcome these obstacles and unlock the benefits of containerization for their legacy applications. By leveraging Docker's platform and ecosystem of tools and services, organizations can modernize existing workflows, streamline application deployment processes, and improve the scalability, agility, and resilience of containerized legacy systems. Continuous innovation and collaboration within the Docker community ensure that organizations have access to the latest technologies and best practices for containerizing legacy applications and driving digital transformation initiatives forward.

Chapter 9: DevOps Practices for Dockerized Microservices

Continuous Integration and Deployment (CI/CD) pipelines are essential components of modern software development practices, particularly in the context of microservices architectures. These pipelines automate the process of building, testing, and deploying microservices, enabling organizations to deliver high-quality software at scale with increased speed and efficiency. Docker, with its lightweight containers and ecosystem of tools, plays a crucial role in enabling CI/CD pipelines for microservices.

The first step in setting up a CI/CD pipeline for microservices is to define the pipeline stages and workflow. This typically involves creating a configuration file, such as a YAML file, to specify the build, test, and deployment steps for each microservice. Tools like Jenkins, GitLab CI/CD, or Travis CI are commonly used for defining and orchestrating CI/CD pipelines. Once the pipeline configuration is defined, developers can commit their code changes to version control, triggering the CI/CD pipeline to automatically build and test the microservices.

To integrate Docker into the CI/CD pipeline, developers typically use Dockerfiles to define the build environment and dependencies for each microservice. Dockerfiles are simple text files that contain instructions for building Docker images, such as installing dependencies, copying application code, and exposing network ports. By encapsulating the build environment within Docker containers, developers can ensure consistent and reproducible builds across different environments, from development to production.

Once the Docker images are built, the next stage in the CI/CD pipeline is to run automated tests to validate the functionality and performance of the microservices. This may include unit tests, integration tests, and end-to-end tests to verify that the microservices behave as expected and meet the specified requirements. Tools like JUnit, Selenium, and Postman are commonly used for writing and running automated tests in CI/CD pipelines. Docker containers provide an isolated and controlled environment for running tests, ensuring that tests are executed consistently and reliably across different environments.

After the automated tests pass successfully, the final stage in the CI/CD pipeline is to deploy the microservices to production or staging environments. Docker provides several options for deploying containerized applications, including Docker Swarm, Kubernetes, and cloud-based container orchestration platforms like Amazon ECS and Google Kubernetes Engine (GKE). These platforms enable organizations to deploy microservices in a scalable, resilient, and automated manner, with features such as service discovery, load balancing, and auto-scaling.

In addition to deploying microservices to production environments, CI/CD pipelines often include additional stages for monitoring and logging to ensure the health and performance of the deployed microservices. Tools like Prometheus, Grafana, and ELK stack (Elasticsearch, Logstash, and Kibana) are commonly used for monitoring and logging in CI/CD pipelines. By integrating monitoring and logging into the CI/CD pipeline, organizations can proactively identify and troubleshoot issues in real-time, ensuring the reliability and availability of their microservices.

Overall, CI/CD pipelines are essential for enabling continuous integration and deployment of microservices, allowing organizations to deliver software updates quickly, reliably, and with confidence. By leveraging Docker containers and associated tools in the CI/CD pipeline, organizations can streamline the software development lifecycle, accelerate time-to-market, and improve overall software quality. Continuous innovation and automation in CI/CD pipelines enable organizations to stay competitive in today's fast-paced digital landscape, delivering value to customers faster and more efficiently than ever before.

Monitoring and logging are crucial aspects of managing Dockerized microservices, providing insights into application performance, health, and security. Docker offers various tools and techniques to facilitate effective monitoring and logging strategies, enabling organizations to gain visibility into their containerized environments and troubleshoot issues proactively.

One fundamental aspect of monitoring Dockerized microservices is collecting metrics and logs from containers and orchestrators. Docker provides a built-in logging driver mechanism that allows administrators to configure where container logs are sent. The **docker run** command can be used to specify the logging driver and destination, such as stdout, stderr, or a logging driver plugin like Fluentd or Splunk. For example, to run a container with JSON-file logging driver, you can use the following command:

perlCopy code

```
docker run --log-driver=json-file my-container
```

In addition to Docker's built-in logging capabilities, organizations often leverage external logging solutions to centralize logs from multiple containers and hosts. Tools like ELK stack (Elasticsearch, Logstash, and Kibana), Fluentd, and Splunk are commonly used for log aggregation and analysis in Dockerized environments. These tools enable administrators to search, filter, and visualize logs, helping to identify trends, anomalies, and potential issues.

Monitoring containerized applications involves tracking various metrics related to resource usage, performance, and availability. Docker provides a built-in monitoring tool called Docker Stats, which displays real-time metrics for CPU, memory, and network usage of running containers. The **docker stats** command can be used to view container resource usage, as shown below:

Copy code

```
docker stats
```

In addition to Docker Stats, organizations often use external monitoring solutions like Prometheus, Grafana, and Datadog for comprehensive monitoring of Dockerized microservices. These tools enable administrators to collect, store, and visualize metrics from containers and orchestrators, allowing them to monitor performance, detect anomalies, and trigger alerts based on predefined thresholds.

Container orchestration platforms like Docker Swarm and Kubernetes also include built-in monitoring and logging capabilities. Docker Swarm provides a built-in monitoring and logging stack called Docker Monitoring and Logging (DML), which integrates with external monitoring solutions like Prometheus and Grafana. Similarly, Kubernetes includes a built-in monitoring solution called kube-state-metrics, which collects metrics from Kubernetes clusters and exposes them in a format that can be consumed by monitoring tools.

To deploy monitoring and logging solutions in Dockerized environments, organizations typically use containerized versions of these tools. Docker Compose or Kubernetes manifests can be used to define and deploy monitoring and logging stacks as Docker services or Kubernetes deployments. For example, a Docker Compose file can define services for Prometheus, Grafana, and Alertmanager, as shown below:

yamlCopy code

version: '3' services: prometheus: image: prom/prometheus ports: - "9090:9090" volumes: - ./prometheus.yml:/etc/prometheus/prometheus.yml grafana: image: grafana/grafana ports: - "3000:3000" environment: - GF_SECURITY_ADMIN_PASSWORD=admin

Once deployed, administrators can access the monitoring and logging dashboards provided by these tools to gain insights into containerized environments, diagnose issues, and optimize performance. By adopting effective monitoring and logging strategies, organizations can ensure the reliability, availability, and performance of their Dockerized microservices, ultimately delivering better user experiences and driving business success.

Chapter 10: Advanced Monitoring and Troubleshooting Strategies

Advanced monitoring and troubleshooting strategies are essential for maintaining the health, performance, and security of containerized environments. With the complexity introduced by microservices architectures and container orchestration platforms like Docker Swarm and Kubernetes, organizations need sophisticated tools and techniques to effectively monitor and troubleshoot issues.

One advanced monitoring strategy is to implement distributed tracing, which allows organizations to track requests as they propagate through multiple microservices. Distributed tracing tools like Jaeger and Zipkin enable administrators to visualize the flow of requests across services, identify latency bottlenecks, and troubleshoot performance issues. These tools rely on instrumentation libraries added to microservices code to generate trace data, which is then aggregated and analyzed to provide insights into application behavior.

To deploy distributed tracing in a Dockerized environment, administrators can use dedicated tracing agents deployed as sidecar containers alongside application containers. These agents intercept incoming and outgoing requests, generate trace data, and forward it to a central tracing backend for analysis. For example, to deploy Jaeger as a tracing backend in a Kubernetes cluster, administrators can use Helm to install the Jaeger Operator and configure it to collect trace data from applications.

Another advanced monitoring strategy is to implement anomaly detection and predictive analytics to proactively identify and mitigate potential issues before they impact production environments. Machine learning-based anomaly detection tools like Prometheus Anomaly Detection and Outlier Detection in Grafana can analyze historical performance metrics to establish baselines and detect deviations indicative of abnormal behavior. By setting up alerting rules based on these deviations, organizations can be notified of potential issues in real-time and take proactive measures to address them.

In addition to monitoring application performance, organizations must also monitor the security posture of their containerized environments. Security monitoring tools like Sysdig Secure and Aqua Security provide real-time threat detection, vulnerability scanning, and compliance auditing for Dockerized workloads. These tools integrate with existing logging and monitoring solutions to correlate security events with performance metrics and provide a holistic view of container security.

Effective troubleshooting in containerized environments requires comprehensive visibility into application behavior, system metrics, and network traffic. Container-specific troubleshooting tools like

Docker Enterprise Edition (EE) and Kubernetes Dashboard provide insights into container lifecycle events, resource utilization, and networking configuration. Administrators can use these tools to diagnose issues, troubleshoot performance bottlenecks, and perform root cause analysis.

Furthermore, organizations can leverage log aggregation platforms like ELK stack (Elasticsearch, Logstash, and Kibana) and Splunk to centralize logs from containers, hosts, and orchestrators for comprehensive troubleshooting. These platforms enable administrators to search, filter, and visualize logs across distributed environments, facilitating rapid troubleshooting and resolution of issues.

To summarize, advanced monitoring and troubleshooting strategies are essential for maintaining the reliability, availability, and security of containerized environments. By implementing distributed tracing, anomaly detection, security monitoring, and comprehensive troubleshooting tools, organizations can effectively monitor, diagnose, and resolve issues in Dockerized and Kubernetes environments, ensuring the optimal performance of their microservices applications.

Advanced monitoring and troubleshooting strategies play a crucial role in ensuring the smooth operation of containerized environments, particularly in the context of modern microservices architectures. These architectures, characterized by their distributed nature and dynamic scaling capabilities, introduce unique challenges in terms of monitoring, diagnosing, and resolving issues.

One key aspect of advanced monitoring is the implementation of service mesh architectures, such as Istio and Linkerd. Service meshes provide advanced observability features like distributed tracing, metrics collection, and traffic management. By deploying a sidecar proxy alongside each microservice instance, service meshes can intercept and monitor all traffic flowing between services. This allows for detailed insights into communication patterns, latency, and error rates across the entire microservices ecosystem.

Deploying a service mesh involves configuring the proxy sidecars to intercept traffic, collecting telemetry data, and forwarding it to a centralized control plane for analysis. Tools like Istio's Prometheus and Grafana integrations can then be used to visualize metrics, create dashboards, and set up alerting rules based on predefined thresholds. Additionally, service mesh data can be correlated with application logs and infrastructure metrics to gain a comprehensive understanding of system behavior.

Another advanced monitoring technique is the use of synthetic monitoring and chaos engineering practices. Synthetic monitoring involves simulating user interactions with applications by generating artificial traffic to assess performance and availability. By deploying synthetic monitoring agents within containerized environments, organizations can proactively identify potential issues before they impact end users. Chaos engineering, on the other hand, involves intentionally injecting failures and disruptions into production systems to test their resilience. Tools like Gremlin and Chaos Mesh enable organizations to conduct controlled experiments to validate system reliability and recovery mechanisms.

In addition to monitoring, advanced troubleshooting techniques involve analyzing application logs, system metrics, and network traffic to diagnose issues accurately. Log aggregation platforms like Fluentd and Logstash can collect logs from various sources, including containers, hosts, and applications, and forward them to centralized repositories for analysis. By correlating logs with metrics and tracing data, administrators can quickly pinpoint the root cause of performance degradations, errors, and failures.

Furthermore, advanced troubleshooting often requires the use of debugging and profiling tools to gain insights into application internals. For example, tools like Telepresence and Skaffold enable developers to debug microservices running in Kubernetes clusters locally by establishing transparent proxies and redirecting traffic to development environments. Profiling tools like pprof and Java Flight Recorder can be used to analyze CPU, memory, and I/O usage within containerized applications to identify performance bottlenecks and optimize resource utilization.

Overall, advanced monitoring and troubleshooting are essential components of modern containerized environments, particularly in the context of microservices architectures. By leveraging service meshes, synthetic monitoring, chaos engineering, log aggregation, and debugging tools, organizations can ensure the reliability, availability, and performance of their containerized applications in production environments.

Conclusion

In summary, the "Docker: Zero to Hero" book bundle offers a comprehensive journey from the fundamentals of containerization to mastering advanced techniques and deployment strategies. Through four meticulously crafted books, readers are equipped with the knowledge and skills needed to harness the power of Docker for building, testing, and deploying applications with speed and efficiency.

"Book 1 - Docker Demystified: A Beginner's Guide to Containerization" lays the foundation by introducing readers to the basic concepts of Docker and containerization. From understanding Docker architecture to creating and managing containers, this book provides a clear and accessible introduction to the world of containers for beginners.

"Book 2 - Mastering Docker: Advanced Techniques and Best Practices" dives deeper into Docker's advanced features and best practices. Readers learn how to optimize Docker images, implement networking and storage solutions, and orchestrate multi-container applications using Docker Compose. With a focus on scalability, security, and performance, this book equips readers with the expertise to leverage Docker effectively in production environments.

"Book 3 - Docker Deployment Strategies: Scaling and Orchestrating Containers" explores the intricacies of deploying Docker containers at scale. From setting up Docker Swarm clusters to implementing rolling updates and service scaling, this book provides insights into orchestrating containerized applications for high availability and resilience. Readers also learn about advanced networking and security considerations for deploying Docker in production.

"Book 4 - Expert Docker: Building Complex Microservices Architectures" delves into the realm of microservices architecture and demonstrates how Docker can be used to build and deploy complex, distributed systems. With a focus on designing scalable, resilient, and maintainable microservices architectures, this book equips readers with the knowledge and tools to architect and deploy sophisticated containerized applications.

Collectively, these four books provide a comprehensive and practical guide for individuals and teams looking to master Docker and accelerate their journey from zero to hero in containerization. Whether you're a novice seeking to grasp the fundamentals or an experienced practitioner aiming to optimize your Docker workflows, this book bundle offers valuable insights and techniques to help you succeed in today's fast-paced world of software development and deployment.